‘The sea has never been friendly to mankind. At best it has been the accomplice of human restlessness.’

Joseph Conrad

Publishers Note

The views and opinions expressed in this book are those of the author entirely by whom they are honestly held. Readers should draw their own conclusions about any claims made or facts and opinions stated or reproduced, concerning which the possibility of alternative perspectives, narratives, descriptions and interpretations should be borne in mind.

THE FORGOTTEN SHIPWRECK

Solving the Mystery of the *Darlwyne*

Nick Lyon

ISBN 978-1-909455-31-3 (Paperback)
ISBN 978-1-909455-32-0 (EPUB ebook)
ISBN 978-1-909455-33-7 (PDF ebook)

Cataloguing-In-Publication Data A catalogue record for this book can be obtained from the British Library.

Published 2019 by

Dived Up Publications
Oxford • United Kingdom
Email info@divedup.com
Web DivedUp.com

Contents

About the author

Nick Lyon was born in Plymouth, to seafaring parents, and has had a lifelong passion for the sea. Inspired as a child by the films of Jacques Cousteau, he snorkelled the coastline of Devon and Cornwall until, in 1982, he learned to scuba dive. He went on to obtain numerous diving and instructor qualifications from the British Sub-Aqua Club and the Nautical Archaeology Society, among others. He has twice been awarded the Alan Broadhurst award for conducting underwater rescues. In 2010, he gave up a 28-year career as a Senior Operating Theatre Practitioner in the NHS, in order to write, drive boats and dive full time. He has appeared on television and radio numerous times, talking about his various wreck hunting projects. For eight years, he wrote a monthly column in *SCUBA* magazine and is still a regular contributor. This is Nick's second book, his first is *The Diver's Tale* (2019, 2nd Edn, Dived Up Publications). He now lives in the Orkney Islands with his wife Julie and dog Skipper.

Foreword

I missed the opportunity to write the Foreword to Nick's last book, *A Diver's Tale* and, in order to alleviate my guilt, I jumped at the chance to pen this one. Little did I know that Nick is a master of both comedy and tragedy and this was to be the latter.

Like most British divers, I love a shipwreck … and a good story. I remember my first wreck dive back in 1991 on the *James Egan Lane* which was torpedoed in World War II near Plymouth. Luckily, she sank with no loss of life and all on board made it to shore. She now has another purpose as an artificial reef at the bottom of the sea. Swimming amongst the fish that shoal around the still-intact bow, you can't help but wonder what the feeling was on board as the reality of her sinking became apparent; the panic that would have set in and how the crew managed to reach the safety of the land.

I have spent many exhilarating dives exploring and filming British wrecks, from First World War U-boats to wooden, medieval cargo vessels; delving into the history and stories behind how they sank; working with expert divers and historians to piece together new evidence and re-writing the stories of how they met their untimely ends.

But this tale is different: this is an event that happened in living memory — a tragic accident on a pleasure craft that could have so easily been avoided. A sobering tale of deceit, lies and greed which cost the lives of 31 innocent people.

I read it from cover to cover, on a wet morning in a tent in Alderney. The rain didn't let up all day and I felt overshadowed by the feeling of sadness at the unnecessary loss of life. Walking along the coast that evening, I thought of those innocent people who trusted in the crew and the vessel to bring them safely back home.

Nick narrates this meticulously-researched story, by carefully and clearly presenting the evidence; weaving the various threads together before finally bringing the tale to a climax. Filling in the gaps with careful and well-judged assumptions, he recounts the probable sequence of events which brought the Darlwyne to her untimely end. But, did he finally locate the site of the wreck and provide some closure for relatives? Could this be the perfect end to a tragic tale? Read on to find out … and good on you, Nick.

Miranda Krestovnikoff
September 2019

The author of the Foreword

Miranda Krestovnikoff is a TV presenter, author and diver. She has presented television and radio stories around the world, on environmental issues, travel and wreck diving, amongst other things. She is also President of the Royal Society for the Protection of Birds (RSPB), patron of Alderney Wildlife Trust, patron of Whale and Dolphin Conservation (WDC), honorary life patron of the Shark Conservation Society, Sea Champion of the Marine Conservation Society and one of the first Friends of the Canal & River Trust.

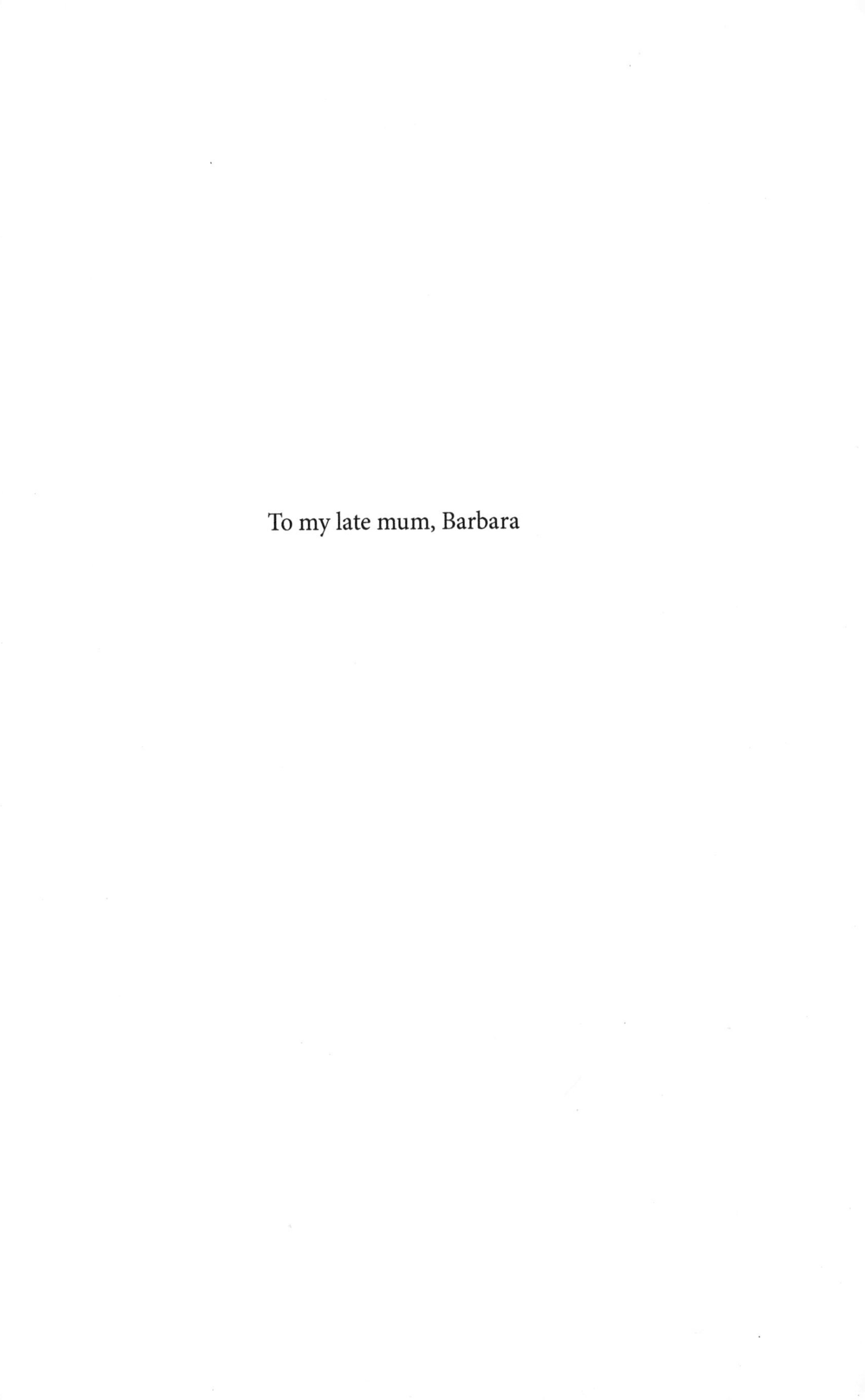

To my late mum, Barbara

TRURO
St Ives
Mylor
St Maw
Falmouth
Zone Point
Penzance
Helston
Land's End
Manacle Point
Lizard
Lizard Point

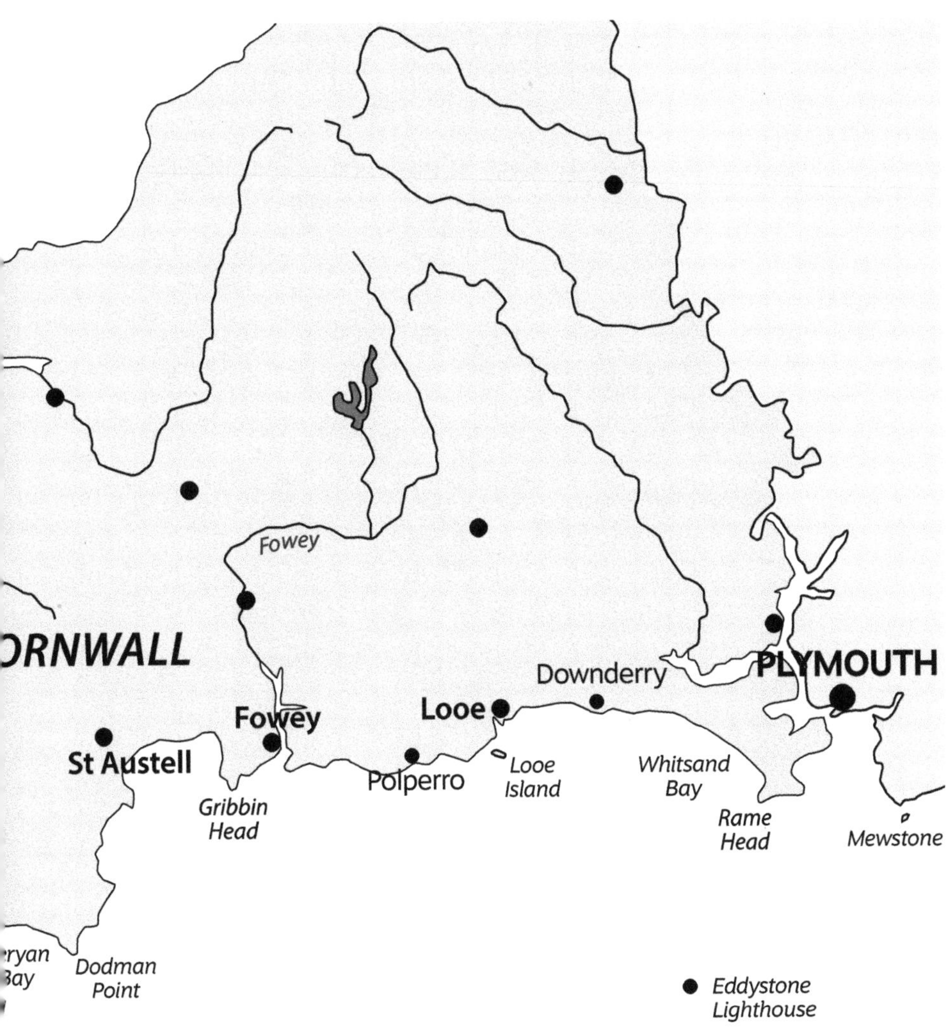

English Channel

Introduction

On Thursday, the 4th of August 1966, the sea began to give up its dead. The bodies of Amanda Hicks, aged 17 from Mylor in Cornwall, Albert Russel, 50, his wife Margaret, 47, from Southport, and Susan Tassell aged 14 from Barnet, were discovered floating some four miles east of Dodman Point on the south coast of Cornwall. The following day, the body of 24-year-old Jean Brock from Halifax was found, wearing a ship's lifebuoy. She had been eight months pregnant. Three days later, on the 8th of August, Margaret Wright aged 22 from London, and her sister, Susan Cowan, 14 from Sunderland, were discovered some distance apart in the vicinity of the Eddystone Reef. On the 10th of August, Patricia Russel, 19, the daughter of Albert and Margaret, was located some six miles to the south of Looe Island, while Eileen Tassell, Susan Tassell's mother, was found close to the Plymouth Mewstone. On the 11th of August, the body of Janice Mills 9, from Southport, came ashore in Whitsand Bay and two days later, on the 13th, her brother David, aged 11, was washed up nearby at Downderry. Three days later on the 16th of August, Janice and David's father, Arthur Raymond Mills, aged 42, was discovered about ten miles from the Mewstone.

For their relatives, friends and communities, the unimaginable grief could at least be tempered to some small extent by the fact that their remains had been found. For the loved ones of 19 other people, there was to be no such closure. All 31 lives were lost because they had been aboard a small boat which foundered in a storm off the south coast of Cornwall. The name of the boat was the *Darlwyne.*

For the small village of Mylor near Falmouth, the death of Amanda Hicks and Joel, her 9-year-old brother who was never found, was the tip of a tragic iceberg. Of the 31 passengers, 27 were staying at the Greatwood Hotel in the village.

1966 was a year marked by relative prosperity and optimism. Ownership of the two most desirable status symbols of the day — a television set and a car — were on the increase and they informed and mobilised the population of Britain as never before. Private boat ownership grew too, particularly in coastal areas with naval connections, as the Royal Navy regularly sold off its glut of small craft at bargain prices. My own father began a lifetime of boat ownership by purchasing a ship's boat formerly belonging to HMS *Vanguard* in 1963. These vessels were built to a very high standard, although they were sometimes modified for the leisure sector with considerably less craftsmanship in evidence (not in my father's case, I should add), as we shall see.

Earlier in the year, Prime Minister Harold Wilson's Labour Government had the slenderest of majorities in the House of Commons. Wilson gambled on an early general election and raised his majority to over 90. Always media savvy, Wilson was very much seen as a man of the people. His Gannex raincoat and his pipe were to become his trademark. In fact, he preferred cigars, but never smoked them in public for fear of damaging his humble image. He made sure he was filmed with the Beatles, despite being incredulous at their popularity, and holidayed on the Isles of Scilly, which only served to emphasize the impression that he was down to earth and far removed from the aloof, aristocratic prime ministers of old.[1] This period undoubtedly saw the real flowering of political spin, decades before Bernard Ingham and Alistair Campbell became as well-known as Margaret Thatcher and Tony Blair, the respective prime ministers whose images they carefully crafted. But one of the key tricks in the arsenal of

1. *Harold Wilson*, Ben Pimlott, BCA 1992.

the modern political spin doctor was to inadvertently colour the story of the *Darlwyne*, namely the concept of the 'bad news day'.

Nowadays, it has become common practice for a politician to disguise a political misjudgement or a personal indiscretion by keeping such disclosure back until a much more absorbing story will capture the public imagination and the bad news will go relatively unnoticed and soonest forgotten, 'tomorrow's chip wrapper' as such disposable copy was termed. So it was, albeit unwittingly, with the *Darlwyne*. She sank on the evening of the 31st of July 1966. The previous day, the England football team had beaten West Germany by four goals to two in a thrilling World Cup Final at Wembley Stadium. The euphoria which followed served to effectively overshadow the news of the *Darlwyne* tragedy, with the result that outside of the communities directly affected it has now all but disappeared from the national consciousness.

Even amongst seafarers, the period of respectful mourning regarding the tragedy was short lived. In the November 1966 issue of *Sea Breezes* magazine for example, the writer Robert Simper bemoaned the fact that the increased scrutiny from the Board of Trade following the *Darlwyne* sinking meant that the crews in a barge race around Harwich harbour would have to be reduced to twelve to comply with regulations. The implication being that before the *Darlwyne* event, this rule may have been regularly flouted for competitive advantage. In an act of similar insensitivity, the *Daily Express* in January 1967 reported the distress of one Alan Mays-Smith, who was the organizer of the annual Oxford v Cambridge boat race. The passenger boats which followed the race boats were not given exemption from the regulations which had been so disastrously broken in the case of the *Darlwyne* and Mr Mays-Smith complained: '... I think we must be prepared to be restricted to twelve in each launch. And with half a dozen coaches in each I foresee an awful row'.[2]

The massive search for the *Darlwyne* was soon scaled down. Those touched by the tragedy lived their lives in private grief and remembrance. When Megan Cardew Rawling, formerly Hicks, the mother of Amanda

2. *Daily Express*, Thursday, 26th January 1967.

and her brother Joel, died in Falmouth Hospital in 2004, aged 79, she was interred with her daughter in the beautiful churchyard at Mylor, and the local connection with the *Darlwyne* tragedy seemingly died with her.

But the tale of the *Darlwyne* was not completely over. For those of us who hunt for shipwrecks, our quest is not always for treasure. More often than not it's to tell a forgotten story, and I had never encountered one like this before. It is a story which spans so many facets, from a village numbed by grief and whole families wiped out, to angry exchanges in the House of Commons and the courts. There is intrigue, chicanery, deceit, incompetence, and greed. But for all this, it's a story which lacks an ending.

In 2016, a group of divers, archaeologists, film makers, photographers and wreck researchers decided that the tale needed to be taken to its natural conclusion. I was part of that group and this is what we found.

Nick Lyon

‘If a man must be obsessed by something, I suppose a boat is as good as anything, perhaps a bit better than most. A small sailing craft is not only beautiful, it is seductive and full of strange promise and the hint of trouble.’

E B White

CHAPTER 1

Origin

There came a point in the development of naval ships when their very size put them at something of a disadvantage. By the latter half of the 19th century, any warship worthy of the name would rely on smaller boats, some of which were carried on board, to perform those tasks which called for speed and manoeuvrability. These small vessels varied enormously in their designs and the roles which they undertook. For much of their history they were powered by steam and examples of such craft are still sought out by collectors of classic boats to this day. Although despite the fact that between 1867 and 1939 over 1,000 small steam boats were built for the Royal Navy, very few now survive.[1] Some vessels acted purely as water taxis to transport crew members to ships at anchor rather than alongside a quay or jetty. These fell under the general, though not exclusive, description of a pinnace.

Others performed a greater variety of duties. Not only would they transport personnel, but stores as well, and they had another, more aggressive role. Some were even fitted with a small gun in order to fulfil their task of maintaining a security perimeter around ships at anchor. This perimeter was known as a picket line, and the boats, picket boats. In the French navy, such a vessel was called a *vedette* which translates to

1. *Steam Picket Boats*, Lt Cmdr. N B J Stapleton, Terence Dalton, 1980.

'picket' too. This term was also taken up by the Royal Navy and, by 1870, was in common usage alongside other terms for these craft. These vessels all fell under the general description of 'ships' boats'.

The picket boat was used by all the world's major navies, but evolved widely according to the circumstances in which it was used. In the United States, for example, some Civil War era picket boats were fitted with spar torpedoes which effectively turned the boat into a floating bomb on a stick. Interestingly, when these were deployed they were often too corroded to function correctly, much to the relief of the crews of the ships which they rammed! In the era of prohibition (1920–1933), the American navy commissioned over 500 picket boats to intercept the rum runners who delivered illegal alcohol from larger ships to small coastal communities.

In Great Britain, where prohibition was thankfully unthinkable, the Royal Navy also developed a more combative role for its picket boats. From 1886, many were armed with a Hotchkiss 3-pounder gun or other short-range weapons to offer a fast, flexible gun platform.[2]

By the outbreak of the Second World War, the picket boat was an indispensable part of every major naval force. A common naval saying was, 'A midshipman's place is in the boats'. Nowadays the Royal Navy maintains just one small fleet of P1000, 12.8 metre picket boats at the Britannia Royal Naval College at Dartmouth in Devon, and they are still the first command of every aspiring Royal Navy officer, including HRH Prince William.[3] But for all their ubiquity, the picket boat had its limitations. Primarily, they were not designed to be seagoing vessels: their area of normal operation being restricted to harbours and estuaries, only venturing further out to sea when conditions were suitably calm. Nevertheless, the Royal Navy had an insatiable appetite for such craft.

In 1893, four boatyards were invited to tender for the construction of a 55-foot steam pinnace which would have cost the Royal Navy £2,500, but this was small change compared with what was to follow. Just three years later, in 1896, the Royal Navy invited 19 boatyards to tender for the

2. *Steam Picket Boats,* Lt Cmdr. N B J Stapleton, Terence Dalton, 1980.
3. 'By the Dart' website https://www.bythedart.co.uk/about-dartmouth/britannia-royal-naval-college---picket-boats/

construction of the following:

Eleven 56-foot steam pinnaces;
Six 52½-foot harbour launches;
Thirty-six 40-foot steam pinnaces;
Five 40-foot admiral's barges;
Twenty-four 32-foot steam cutters;
Two 32-foot admiral's barges;
Twelve 27-foot steam cutters;
Six 23-foot steam cutters.

Between 1895 and 1902 alone, tenders were invited for the construction of 433 ships' boats.[4]

At the outbreak of the First World War, the Royal Navy had some 442 fighting ships, all requiring ships' boats. By the start of the Second World War, that number had fallen to 367, as submarines and aircraft carriers had come along to enhance the fighting capability of the service. Nevertheless, the demand for small boats was extremely high and hundreds of boatyards submitted tenders to supply the Admiralty. Just in the small Cornish town of Looe, for example, there were three such yards. So vital were these small shipbuilders to the war effort, that those who worked in them were deemed to be in a reserved occupation and were therefore exempt from conscription into the armed forces. By this time, it was common for boats to be ordered in pairs so that one was always available while the other was undergoing maintenance or repairs, so it's little wonder that boatyards were keen to win such lucrative orders.

So, it was by this process that in 1941, the Shoreham Yacht Works boatyard of Shoreham-by-Sea in Sussex submitted a tender to build a 45-foot medium speed picket boat, which was accepted by the Admiralty. To be precise, her length was actually a carefully measured 45 feet, nine and ¼ inch. At her widest, her beam was to be eleven feet, four inches and from keel to gunwale was six feet one inch. She drew a maximum of three feet.[5] The specification called for double diagonal construction, which was the

4. *Steam Picket Boats,* Lt Cmdr. N B J Stapleton, Terence Dalton, 1980.
5. Report of Court No. 8046, M.V. Darlwyne.

norm for his type of vessel at that time.

The term 'double diagonal' refers to the way in which hull planking is laid. It consists of two layers of thin planks, in this case of 5⁄16 inch or 3⁄8 inch strips of African mahogany, laid at right angles in a diagonal orientation. This gives great strength for minimal weight. It was normal for the Admiralty to specify that a layer of calico soaked in boiled linseed oil (linseed oil is highly flammable if not boiled) be inserted between the two layers as an extra defence against leaking. It is unclear whether in the case of this particular vessel that was actually included. The frames were of rock elm, one and ¼ by ⅞ inch in sections every seven inches with additional strength coming from five stringers per side and web frames every fourth timber. Strong though it was, this type of construction was highly technical and labour intensive. A boat of this size could require upwards of 20,000 copper nails in the hull alone.[6] In order to accommodate the curvature of the hull, these vessels were usually built starting in the middle and extending outwards to the bow and stern. As we shall see, despite its strength there was also a major disadvantage of the double diagonal design.

The vessel in question was to be fitted with twin Gardner 6LW diesel engines which could develop 95 horsepower at 1,600 revs. Internally, there were to be four fully watertight bulkheads and two described as 'semi watertight' that is, the bulkheads nearest the bow and the stern were fitted with valves which could be opened or closed to allow drainage or ventilation. The steering was configured such that the twin rudders would move from amidships to fully over with one turn of the wheel.

On completion of the build, the vessel was handed over to the Admiralty who gave it the service number 41768. She undertook the normal duties of a picket boat for the duration of the Second World War for the Royal Navy and was occasionally loaned to the United States Navy too. It was later claimed that, when she was used by the US navy, she would carry 100 men at a time, although this claim now sounds decidedly fanciful and

---

6. Author interview with Andy Skentelbery, a traditional boat builder who served his apprenticeship constructing, among other things, picket boats.

a maximum of around 40 was the more usual number.

Following the war, she was used less intensively and eventually became surplus to requirements. In 1957 the Admiralty put her up for sale at Gosport in Hampshire when she was purchased by the Belsize Boat Yard of Southampton for £600. Mr W E Smith, a director of the yard later said that at that price she was: '... one of the most expensive [ex-Admiralty boats] we ever bought. We thought from that price she must be a fairly good boat.'[7]

It was here that she underwent significant and, in the light of future events, critical alteration. In order to make her more commercially attractive, the vessel was converted into a cabin cruiser. Crucially, five of the six bulkheads were removed, the exception being the one at the forward end of the engine compartment. They were replaced with four new bulkheads, none of which were watertight.

In 1959, having completed her refit, the boat was sold by Belsize Boatyard to Graham P Lowe and Geoffrey J Gray of Uxbridge Road, London jointly for the sum of £1,689 which equates to approximately £38,603 in 2018.[8] The new owners immediately had the old Gardner engines replaced with Perkins P6 engines which developed 86 horsepower at 2,600 revs (this figure was actually reported as 65 horsepower at 2,000 revs in the court of inquiry). They were direct drive engines, which did not require a gear box, and were of a smaller size than the original engines, as were the propellers. They were placed some 18 inches further forward than the Gardner engines. Interestingly, these engines were too powerful for the hull in which they were fitted, as a boat's maximum speed is dictated as much by the design of the hull as the power of the engines.

At 12.35 tons displacement, she fell under the minimum size of 50 tons, which would have required compulsory registration. Nevertheless, on Friday the 22nd of April 1960, Lowe and Gray registered the boat formerly known as simply 41768 on the mercantile navy list, as number 301110 and with a proper name. They called her the *Darlwyne*.

7. *The Times*, 14th December 1966.
8. Using the Bank of England's inflation calculator.

The origin of the name is something of a mystery. Even acknowledged *Darlwyne* expert Martin Banks has yet to discover what it actually means. In various reports, newspaper articles and newsreel films it is more often than not misspelled as 'Darlwin', 'Darlwyn', 'Darlwynne', or even 'Darwin'. It may be that it comes from the amalgamation of two names which were significant to Lowe and Gray. It would certainly have caused some confusion nowadays when vessels are so often called upon to broadcast their identity via VHF radio, a piece of equipment which was never available on the *Darlwyne*. It later transpired that some confusion even arose within the family of a subsequent owner, as the name was spelled two different ways when emblazoned on the boat itself.

Lowe and Gray had the *Darlwyne* moved to Teddington in Middlesex to be used as a cabin cruiser on the River Thames. This could be why she was registered on the mercantile list, as it may have smoothed the way for the acquisition of the required permits to operate on the river. It is not clear whether she was transported by road or sea, but moving a boat of her size by road was less common then than it would be now, and a sea voyage seems the more likely option.

Either way, in October of 1962, Lowe decided that the *Darlwyne* was to undertake her first recorded sea voyage when she was sailed out of the Thames Estuary and westward along the English Channel to St Mawes on the Percuil River in Cornwall. She would remain in Cornwall for the rest of her days. She was crewed by six people and skippered by an experienced St Mawes man named John Edward Green, a carpenter by trade. Although the passage was completed without incident, it acted, in effect, as a sea trial for the *Darlwyne* and it was a voyage which highlighted some issues with the boat.

This was the first time that difficulty with the steering was recorded. It was said to be far too light, particularly with the wind on the beam. High windage, that is the influence of the wind on the profile of the boat, was also mentioned. Green later described how the *Darlwyne* had: 'Sailed exceptionally well into (the wind) but when the weather came round to the beam she slid and yawed'.[9] Stability concerns were also raised. It was noted that the boat listed easily when the crew moved around her, and the conclusion was drawn that she was short of ballast.

The *Darlwyne* remained in the Percuil River until September 1963 when she was taken across the Fal Estuary to the small harbour at Mylor where she was put up for sale once more. In February 1964, George Corke, a yacht broker, marine surveyor and managing director of Mylor Yacht Harbour, took the *Darlwyne* out into the Fal Estuary to conduct a sea trial for a prospective buyer. He was not impressed. Once again, the steering issues were obvious; in fact it was said to be impossible to steer a straight course. Stability was also a concern, with the shallow draft, lack of bilge keels and high windage being noted once again. Graham Lowe and Geoffrey Gray had asked George Corke to assess the *Darlwyne*'s suitability to be used as a commercial passenger vessel. Of course, as both broker and surveyor, this presented something of a conflict of interests for Corke, but he reported that in his opinion the *Darlwyne* would need a considerable amount of restoration and repair before she could be considered fit for any commercial role.

Notwithstanding his concerns, George Corke had been engaged to sell the *Darlwyne* and that's what he did. A bill of sale dated the 30th of May 1964 records the *Darlwyne* as having been bought by John Campbell Maitland Barratt of Penryn, near Falmouth. In a newspaper interview shortly after the tragedy, George Corke was careful to distance himself from criticism for having brokered the sale of such an unseaworthy boat stating: 'I was acting as an agent. The boat was sold as a yacht for private purposes which could go to sea in certain conditions.' It is unclear whether that corollary was ever mentioned to John Barratt. Tellingly, Corke went on: 'When I sold the boat to Barratt I would have taken it to Fowey myself, but only if I could have chosen the weather'.[10]

John Barratt was a man not unfamiliar with seafaring. In his younger days he had some experience of working with small boats in the Hebrides,

9. *The Times*, 15th December 1966.

10. *The Times*, 16th December 1966.

but by 1964 he had left that far behind. At the time that he bought the *Darlwyne*, he was 59 and described himself as a property development consultant. He was a man with something of a chequered past. He had tried and failed at a number of careers. He was even briefly an officer in the Metropolitan Police, which he joined on the 5th of December 1927 with the warrant number 117018. But the ink had hardly dried on his warrant card when he resigned from the force on the 26th of February 1928.[11] He seems to have been perpetually short of money. As if this wasn't enough, his son had been killed in Malaya and, at the time of the *Darlwyne* tragedy, his wife was seriously ill. He saw the *Darlwyne* as an investment opportunity that would restore his seemingly flagging fortunes. His intention was to renovate her and sell her on at a profit. In an effort to raise the required funds for the renovation, Barratt kept the boat moored alongside the quay at Penryn and let her out as a houseboat.

During the first half of 1965, substantial work was carried out on the *Darlwyne*, much of it by Christopher Mitchell, who was John Barratt's son-in-law. The hull had been repainted following the replacement of some of the timbers. On the 18th of September 1965, John Barratt made a deal with a Steven Gifford to sell the *Darlwyne* to him for £3,000 and the part exchange of another 32-foot cabin cruiser called the *Carpe Diem*, on which there was a £300 mortgage outstanding. Gifford negotiated to make payments of £6 per week.

Gifford immediately began to undertake further work on the *Darlwyne*. The engines were serviced. They were hardly run in, but had not seen much use for quite a while, so this was a sensible move. He also undertook some internal alterations, though exactly who altered what internally is unclear. Of more concern was the state of the hull. Gifford found extensive rot on both sides of the vessel, thereby demonstrating an issue with which the owners of many double diagonally constructed boats will be all too familiar. Strong and light though they undoubtedly are, even with the calico membrane in place (and there is no certainty that the *Darlwyne* had one) there is a tendency for moisture to become trapped between the hull

11. Online Metropolitan Police records, National Archives reference MEPO4/348.

layers, leading to rot.[12] Whether or not this proved too difficult a problem for Steven Gifford to overcome, or whether it has something to do with the fact that around this time he was convicted of theft and fined, he was unwilling or unable to keep up the payments on the *Darlwyne*. So, in the winter of 1965, Barratt repossessed the vessel. At the time of repossession, she was described as looking 'shabby'.

For example, in December 1965, Guy Crossley-Meates of Helford Passage stated that the *Darlwyne*'s deck timbers needing re-caulking and spoke of a serious list when he stepped aboard one day at Custom House Quay in Falmouth. Crossley-Meates singled out 'the poor appearance of the planking and caulking, particularly aft of the after cabin'. Also quoted is the view of John Kingston-Maine who worked as a marine engineer, from Penryn who saw the *Darlwyne* twice. He:

> 'Thought the boat looked "neglected" when he first saw it in Percuil, and when he saw it next in Penryn, he noticed the timbers amidships were "whiskery" as though the boat had been constantly rubbing, with no protection, against a quayside.'[13]

John Barratt realised that there was a great deal to be done in order to make the *Darlwyne* a commercial proposition. His eldest daughter Elizabeth (confusingly, also known as Janet) and her friend, or more likely her boyfriend, Francis (Frank) Lang were enlisted to help, and they set to work with enthusiasm. The hull was scraped of her old paint and re-painted. She was also said to have been re-engined again, but there is some doubt about this given the fact that this had already been done not long before. It seems more likely that the engines were serviced once more. More significantly, there were major alterations to the stern of the boat. The aft cabin was completely removed to leave an open cockpit. This modification would have made the *Darlwyne* a more suitable boat for carrying parties of divers or anglers. To further increase her suitability

12. Author interview with Andy Skentelbery.
13. *Falmouth Packet*, 16th December 1966.

for divers in particular, a gap, two feet six inches wide by one foot high, was cut out of the transom to allow access via a stern-mounted ladder. This gap was closed by a temporary mahogany door.

Francis Lang agreed to work unpaid during the alterations, having been promised back pay once the sale of the *Darlwyne* was complete. It was money he would never receive. He replaced a large amount of hull planking, some 20 feet on both sides of the bow. He commented, as others had done, that the vessel listed very easily. Consequently two and a half tons of pig iron and granite setts (road cobbles) were laid in to increase the ballast to a total of three and a half tons. This was laid more towards the stern as the newer engines were much lighter than the original Gardner models and the boat had a tendency to sit low at the bow. In total, these repairs cost some £886 16s. At this time, Elizabeth Barratt also chemically treated a patch of soft wood near the starboard bow which is indicative of rot in that area.

The court of inquiry into the loss of the *Darlwyne* records that the layout of the vessel on completion of the alterations was as follows:

> 'A forward store with non-watertight bulkhead and door, leading to the forward cabin, partially covered by the coach roof forward.
>
> A door from the forward cabin led to the main cabin which was wholly covered fore and aft by the coach roof. The floor of both cabins was below the waterline.
>
> Aft of these two cabins was the engine room with the only original watertight bulkhead between the spaces. The top of this bulkhead was cut away to allow a ladder to lead to the wheelhouse and hence the bulkhead was only watertight up to approximately 3 feet above the inside of bottom.
>
> On top of the engine compartment was the wheelhouse measuring approximately 8 feet by 8 feet, fitted with large glass windows all round, with doors port and starboard to the weather deck.
>
> Aft, a ladder led down from the wheelhouse to the galley, the floor of which was

at approximately the same level as that of the forward cabins. This ladder again cut into the bulkhead between the galley and the engine room. This galley led, via a fairly substantial teak door to a non-watertight cockpit aft; this was the only portion of the vessel not fully decked. This large open cockpit was approximately 11 feet in length and full breadth except that at deck level there were narrow side decks with a 4-inch coaming extending above deck level. The cockpit was about 18 inches deep and its deck was reasonably watertight at the centre. It was supported on adequate beams which rested on some of the original stringers and the connections to these were not very robust. It was further supported by two longitudinal bearers in turn supported by struts from the original after cabin floor. The cockpit extended at the sides only to the insides of the timbers.

The planking on the central portion was 1 ⅛-inch tongued and grooved with a 3-inch wash strake below and fitted side seats. Outboard of this a 1-inch deck was laid extending to the timbers and this was also fitted with a 3-inch strake against the inside faces of the web frames. As a result there were spaces on each side, giving a total area through which water could drain to the buoyancy space below the cockpit floor of approximately 0.5 square feet per side.

The cockpit floor was constructed to drain off to a small fish box and then through the transom, via a slot approximately 4 inches by 1 inch in area and approximately 15 inches above the load waterline. Two hatches, one 3 feet by 2 feet in area and the other 2 feet by 2 feet in area, were fitted to this cockpit floor and there is reason to believe that these were very tight and safe against lifting, although no safety catches were fitted.

The transom was cut away to facilitate access for divers, etc. via a portable transom ladder to an extent approximately 2 feet 6 inches transversely and one foot vertically. The sides of this slot were formed by Samson posts approximately 4 inches square. Slots were cut into these to allow dropping in a shutter which was approximately 1 inch in thickness and constructed of mahogany.'[14]

14. Report of Court No. 8046, M.V. Darlwyne.

There is a great deal of nautical jargon here (see *Glossary*), but one stark fact is inescapable, namely that, in a boat configured like this, there were a number of ways in which water could enter the hull via the gaps in the deck and, once inside, there were no watertight bulkheads to prevent it flooding the entire hull.

Despite the shortcomings of the internal design of the vessel, it is clear that, at least cosmetically, she was much improved and there was now little sign of neglect. In fact, when the *Darlwyne* story was just beginning to break, Derek McCloud, who owned the jetty in Penryn where the boat was being refitted, was quoted as saying: 'She looked in great shape and could have fetched £6,000.'[15]

As far as John Barratt was concerned, the *Darlwyne* was in good order and ready to go on the open market, and he placed adverts in the local newspapers and national yachting magazines. It would have been extremely difficult to sell a boat without a recent survey report but here John Barratt had a problem. As previously mentioned, he was a man with a seemingly perennial cash flow problem. Luckily for him, his mother, who lived in Scotland, was able to help and she contacted a firm of Edinburgh solicitors called Murray, Beith and Murray (who are still in business today), to arrange a survey. On the 19th of July 1966, George Corke was once again commissioned to conduct a survey on the *Darlwyne*. This small detail turned out to be one of the most tragic twists of fate in the *Darlwyne* story. His report made for unhappy reading:

> 'The boat was in a poor condition. I found damage to the hull 15 feet back from the bows and about 18 inches below the waterline on the starboard side. The hull had also been pushed in. There had been alterations to the boat since I sold her as an agent for Mr Barratt.'[16]

He went on to point out the fact that the new engines were too powerful for the type of hull. This is not a major safety issue, but indicates a lack

15. *Daily Mail*, 2nd August 1966.
16. *The Sun*, 2nd August 1966.

of expertise on the part of those carrying out the re-fit. But although these, and other faults, were carefully catalogued by George Corke, John Barratt never got to see the survey. Quite correctly, Corke returned it to the chambers of Murray, Beith and Murray in Edinburgh since it was they who commissioned it, and there it remained. Enquiries by the author to the law firm regarding the report received no response. We don't know why Barratt's mother didn't collect it or ask for it to be sent on to her son, but the implications of this chain of events are obvious. It may well be that had he been fully aware of the *Darlwyne*'s poor condition, John Barratt might not have let her put to sea. Having said that, he was present, along with his daughter, Elizabeth, and Francis Lang, when the survey was conducted. When George Corke mentioned some of his less welcome findings, Barratt is said to have dismissed them, believing that the hour which Corke took to survey the boat was insufficient to correctly assess the vessel's true condition.

Notwithstanding this, put to sea she did. Various members of Barratt's family used her for short pleasure trips in and around Falmouth Bay. Elizabeth Barratt went to sea in the boat at least twice, once in February and again at Whitsun, which in 1966 fell on the 29th of May, when she sailed to the Helford River, experiencing a force seven wind during the trip. Interestingly, when interviewed, she was keen to point out that in regard to the force seven squall: 'She rode it well and seemed perfectly seaworthy. We had no trouble with her'. She added: 'The dry rot was well above the water line'.[17]

By now John Barratt seems to have been in two minds about selling the *Darlwyne*. Whether this is because there was little interest from potential buyers or he could see more profit in using the boat commercially is unknown. But at this time, it began to be used on a number of short excursions in and around the Falmouth area, and plans were made to take passengers out into Falmouth Bay to view the annual Tall Ships Race.

This particular trip took place on Friday the 8th of July 1966 and the charter was undertaken for a cost of £7, 10 shillings to be split among the

17. The *Daily Mail*, 2nd August 1966.

passengers. The atmosphere on the boat was described by one participant, Elizabeth Pitts, as 'boisterous'. A 16-year-old girl at the time and wearing a bikini, she was subjected to a number of lewd and innuendo-laden comments, seemingly fuelled by the significant amount of alcohol which was consumed during the voyage. Whilst attitudes and social behaviour are different now than they were over 50 years ago, Elizabeth was nevertheless quite uncomfortable about the bawdy behaviour.[18]

18. Author interview with Liz Dunstan (née Pitts).

‘Happiness is brief. It will not stay. God batters at its sails.’

Euripides

CHAPTER 2

A Cast of Characters

Anyone who sets sail from Mylor Yacht Harbour will notice an imposing building protruding through the trees on the left, before they turn south and head down the Fal Estuary towards the open sea. This building, which with its towers and solid stone walls resembles a Scottish castle, is called Greatwood House. These days, it is a luxury apartment complex. But this is not how the building has always been used. The house has a history that is crucial to the village of Mylor in general, and the story of the *Darlwyne* in particular.

The house is situated in 16 acres of land fronted by a shingle beach, and a small quay added in the 18th century. It was built in the 1840s as a private residence by Phillip Daniel, who originated from Trelissick. He died in 1859, and the house passed through a number of owners until in 1895 John Gregory Bond took it on and remained there for some 36 years. In 1936, Greatwood was leased to Major Edward Dorrien-Smith whose time there was marred by tragedy when his daughter died in a car accident and both his sons were killed in action during the Second World War. After Major Dorrien-Smith died, the house was taken over by Captain Gore-Langton and his wife who kept a prize-winning herd of Channel Island cows on the land. In 1961, the Gore-Langton family emigrated to start a new life in Canada and Greatwood House was taken over by a property developer who intended to run it as a 34-room hotel.

The developer was Robert Rainbird.

Rainbird is a character about whom everyone seemed to quickly form an opinion, and that opinion was not always favourable. Indeed, nobody I have managed to trace can find anything good to say about him. Of course it may be that he was a much-maligned character, but I could unearth little evidence to support this. It is known, for example, that he never actually paid for Greatwood House, choosing instead to engage in endless negotiation and procrastination over the money. Not only did he not own his hotel, he ran it without a fire certificate or an alcohol licence, the former having never been issued and the latter having been revoked in May of 1963,[1] despite the fact that his bar was an integral part of the business. It appears he was often in dispute with neighbours and tenants who lived on the estate. On one occasion, he allegedly cut the water main supplying one of the estate cottages following an argument. After another disagreement, he is said to have torched his neighbour's garden with a flame thrower!

Ever keen to boost his income, Robert Rainbird met John Barratt, probably in casual, social circumstances, at some point before the somewhat Bacchanalian excursion to view the Tall Ships Race and suggested that he could supply a steady stream of passengers in the shape of his hotel guests, possibly with the intention of negotiating a share of the profits for himself. Rainbird had certainly been impressed with the *Darlwyne* during the Tall Ships Race trip. He is later quoted as saying that he thought the *Darlwyne* 'handled rather well and could have spun on a sixpence' which is in stark contrast to what we now know about her handling capabilities.[2]

Machiavellian he may or may not have been, but Robert Rainbird was keen to make a success of his hotel business and he worked hard to increase his occupancy rate. In the July of 1966, the hotel was fully booked with guests who had travelled from all over the country to enjoy the idyllic surroundings. Having the capability to offer boat trips was certainly a business advantage for Rainbird, although in the case of the fatal voyage

1. *Falmouth Packet*, 21st April 1967.
2. *Falmouth Packet*, 23rd December 1966.

of the *Darlwyne*, he subsequently went to great lengths to distance himself from any responsibility for the trip, as we shall see.

It was clear to John Barratt that he did not possess sufficient expertise to act as the skipper of the *Darlwyne*, but once again fate was about to intervene in the shape of a 31-year-old carpet salesman from London by the name of Brian Bown. He had considerable maritime experience, having served in the Merchant Navy with the Blue Funnel Line and spent his National Service as a leading aircraftman in the Air Sea Rescue section of the Royal Air Force. He was stationed at RAF Mountbatten in Plymouth to crew the squadron of 63-foot rescue launches known as 'whale tails' because of their unusual curved decks. These were finally decommissioned in 1986 when the ubiquitous Sea King helicopters were recognised as the only sensible means of rescuing downed air crews; but in the early 1960s the squadron was very much an active unit.

Brian Bown was certainly very experienced in Cornish waters from the Isles of Scilly to Plymouth Sound. However, he had turned his back on the sea several years previously to work in the less life-affirming though steadier environment of the East Coast Carpet Stores of Teddington in London. He had probably done this so that his 21-year-old wife, Mary, could continue to work as a model. When Mary became pregnant in early 1966 and put her modelling career on hold, Brian Bown saw an opportunity to return to the kind of work he really enjoyed. He began to put feelers out in the Falmouth area for skippering work. Fiona Mitchell, John Barratt's other daughter, was working at Greatwood and mentioned to Robert Rainbird that her father's boat would soon have a skipper and be ready for charter on behalf of his guests. It seems likely that Brian Bown had already contacted John Barratt, given this turn of events. In fact Francis Lang, who was already a friend of Brian Bown's, had shown him the *Darlwyne* while it was out of the water in a boatyard at Malpas, near Truro. Bown subsequently had a meeting with a Mr Miners of the Falmouth Harbour Commission who gave him a list of the safety equipment required for a commercial vessel. A list of items which, for whatever reason, was ultimately not acquired.

Brian Bown had written a letter to Francis Lang (who seems to have been acting as an agent for John Barratt) dated the 14th of July, indicating that an arrangement was quickly in place. He stated: 'I have decided to accept your offer and will be coming down to run the Darlwin [sic]. I shall be giving a week's notice to East Coast Carpet Stores Ltd'. He added that his employers had: '... offered to transfer me to shop sales at an increase of £2.00 plus commission', but he went on to say that 'selling carpets would drive me up the wall'.[3]

Brian and Mary Bown moved from London to Falmouth on the 25th of July. On the same day, Elizabeth Barratt spent 30 shillings on an order for 25 posters advertising trips on the *Darlwyne* from Borough Printing Works in Penryn, which were ready for collection on the 30th of the month. With the holiday season in full swing, events then moved at a rapid pace in order for the *Darlwyne* to start paying her way as quickly as possible. John Barratt took out a three months, fully comprehensive boat insurance policy with the Eagle Star insurance company, effective from the 20th of July. His daughter Elizabeth personally handed a Lloyds bank cheque for £20 0s 6d to a broker called David Kempthorne-Ley, who verbally assured Barratt the *Darlwyne* was comprehensively insured although there is no cover note or record of any policy to that effect. He had always intended that the boat should be purchased by Brian Bown and they met to discuss this on the 25th. It was intended that a formal sale agreement would be legally formalised in the presence of a solicitor, but this never actually occurred. Confusion over this issue was to form a major part of the subsequent enquiry. Brian Bown had specified that his friend, Jeff Stock, a 35-year-old accountant from Hayle, should be taken on as engineer and crew man and this was agreed. He planned to take the boat to Greatwood on the 30th of July in order to arrange some charters for the hotel guests.

It is at this point that it seems relevant to ask exactly what type of work had Brian Bown intended the *Darlwyne* to undertake? We know that the transom had been partially cut away in order to allow access for divers. On July the 28th he wrote to his wife informing her that he may have secured

3. *Falmouth Packet*, 23rd December 1966.

a booking for a party of twelve divers who were camping at Penzance for the following week, for £75 for the week or £15 per day.[4] But in 1966, membership of the British Sub-Aqua Club (BSAC) stood at just under 8,000, which meant that scuba diving was still very much a minority activity and, by implication, difficult to make a living from.[5] Although sea angling was growing in popularity at the time, with many miles of beautiful coastline and dozens of hotels on the doorstep, the scenic boat trip market seemed the most reliable option.

It seems patently clear that the commercial running of the *Darlwyne* was arranged jointly between John Barratt and Brian Bown. But the question of who exactly organised the fatal voyage of the 31st of July 1966 is harder to answer, and was pivotal to the outcome of the subsequent inquiry. With the posters already printed and skipper and crew engaged, a trip was certainly planned to take place on that date. Brian Bown had already asked a local boatman called David Wakefield a number of questions regarding the regulations regarding the running of a boat for commercial charter. He had even asked Wakefield to place a poster advertising the *Darlwyne* in the foyer of the St Michaels Hotel in Falmouth, but Wakefield had declined to do so until all the legal requirements were met. John Barratt also asked retired Glasgow police sergeant, George Calder, who was managing the Courtenay holiday flats at Swanpool, near Falmouth, to display a poster. Given that Swanpool is on the opposite side of Falmouth from Mylor, it may be that the *Darlwyne* was advertised all over the town.

Exactly what role Robert Rainbird played in the organisation of the trip has never been completely established. What is known is that on the 24th of July, two families arrived at Greatwood, both from Southport on Merseyside, the Mills and the Russels. On the Friday of that week, they had been relaxing on a nearby beach and returned to the hotel for lunch. Rainbird always claimed that it was they, not he, who proposed a boat trip and in response he suggested the *Darlwyne*, although it certainly was he who initially mentioned a fee of £12 for the charter. He telephoned

4. *Falmouth Packet*, 6th January 1967.

5. BSAC website.

Christopher Mitchell, John Barratt's son-in-law (Barratt did not have a telephone) to ask him to come over to the hotel the following evening to make the arrangements.

The two families had spent the early part of the evening of the 30th of July at the Pandora Inn at Mylor Bridge and returned to Greatwood to meet up with Brian Bown and Fiona Mitchell, John Barratt's daughter. She was also accompanied by Francis Lang and John Chard, who had offered to lend a hand as crew. At this point Robert Rainbird announced that the charter price had now increased to £16 per person, returning by 17.00, but for £1 per head, they could have a longer trip lasting until between 18.00 and 19.00. It had also been decided that the destination would be Fowey. By this time, more of the guests had become interested and the numbers of ticketholders had risen to 27. These guests were as follows:

- The Mills family from Southport had holidayed at Greatwood the previous year, which suggests that Robert Rainbird was more restrained in his dealings with his guests than he may have been with his staff. Arthur Raymond (Ray) Mills was 42 and a keen boat owner. He had a speedboat which he used for water skiing on the river Dee. His wife Beryl accompanied him, along with their children David, 11, Janice, 9 and Lisa, 3. Lisa was frightened of the sea, so she was to stay behind at Greatwood with her mother.

- The Russel family were friends of the Mills family and lived close to them. Albert Russel and his wife Margaret were both 50 and comfortably off. They had travelled to Cornwall with their son John, 21, daughter Patricia, 19 and family friend Kenneth Robinson, also 19 from Liverpool. John Russel was in the Merchant Navy, was studying for his second mate's ticket, and he knew the local waters well. Kenneth Robinson was also a merchant seaman, serving as an engineering officer.

- The Tassell Family came from Barnet in London. Peter Lyon Tassell (no relation), 41, was a director of Charrington's Coal

Merchants which still exists, trading as CPL, and has royal patronage. He was accompanied by his wife Eileen, 40, and their children Susan, 14, Nicola, 12, and Frances, 8. The Tassels were a family of practising Catholics and the children attended a convent school. It is particularly tragic that they had planned to go home the previous day but elected to spend an extra night at Greatwood in order to participate in the boat trip.

- The Cowan family came from Sunderland. James Cowan, 52 and his wife Dora, 48, had brought their youngest daughter, 14-year-old Susan. They met up with their son-in-law, Malcolm Wright, and daughter Margaret who lived in London.

- Laurence and Kathleen Bent, 74 and 60, were from Wimbledon in London. They were on holiday with their 20-year-old son, George, and his girlfriend Lorraine Thomas, also 20 from New Maldon in Surrey.

- Roger Brock was a 26-year-old art teacher from Halifax in Yorkshire. With him was his 24-year-old wife, Jean. She was eight months pregnant.

- George Edmonds, 45, came from Derby. He was on holiday with his fiancée Patricia Roome, 48. He was rebuilding his life having tragically lost his wife in a road accident in 1963. Something of a polymath, he was a keen musician and loved sport. He was an engineer at Rolls Royce in Derby. Both he and Patricia had children from their previous marriages.

- Although not on holiday, Mary Rose Dearden was staying at Greatwood whilst working there for the summer season, intending to earn enough money to travel around Portugal. She was 19 and from West Kirby near Liverpool.

- Amanda Hicks, 17, and her brother Joel, 9, lived at Greatwood with their mother, Megan (née Rundle) who worked at the hotel. Originally from Crowlas near Penzance, they had moved to Mylor from Chapel Street in Penzance itself following the death, also at sea, of Megan's husband, Captain Fred Hicks, in 1961.

This is a terribly sad list but, shockingly, it could have been even worse. In the course of researching this book I have traced another nine people who were also booked to participate on the doomed trip.

Chris Rendell, now resident in Mullion, lived in Mylor and was a friend of Joel Hicks. He asked to go on the trip but his grandfather, who was a fisherman, was familiar with the *Darlwyne* and thought her to be unseaworthy. He advised Chris' parents not to let him go and they agreed.[6]

Geraldine (known as Dene) Smith's parents lived some of the time at Greatwood. They owned a pilot cutter called the *Peggy* which they chartered out in the summer and lived on in the winter. Robert Rainbird asked her mother if she and her brother, Jeremy, would like to take part in the trip, but her mother was extremely wary of any scheme which Rainbird might be involved in and declined.[7]

Four teenagers, who asked to remain anonymous, were on holiday from Kent and staying at Polruan, near Fowey. They caught the bus to Fowey and were planning to make the boat trip to Falmouth and return by bus. They were around 16 to 17-years-old. How they came to hear about the trip is unclear. It is possible that some of John Barratt's posters were displayed in Fowey as well as in the Falmouth area. As fate would have it, the teenagers accidentally left their transistor radio at the bus stop and returned to find it. When they finally arrived at Fowey harbour, they saw the *Darlwyne* heading out to sea. They managed to attract Brian Bown's attention, but he is said to have given an exaggerated shrug and stayed on course. In fairness to him, it may well be that, given what we now know about the *Darlwyne*'s poor steering capabilities, turning around to pick

6. Author interview with Chris Rendell.
7. Author interview with Dene Berryman (née Smith).

the teenagers up may have been all but impossible. The witness I spoke to has suffered what would now be called 'survivor guilt' all her life and now lives as something of a recluse.[8]

John Chard, the friend of Brian Bown who had been at the meeting at Greatwood to discuss the trip and who expressed an interest in acting as crew, did not turn up on the Sunday morning. A lecturer in photography at Exeter College, he had known Bown for some six years and later stated his opinion that Bown was both cautious and methodical, so he clearly did not lack confidence in his capabilities.[9]

Similarly, a Mr MacColl, a fisherman from Penryn had originally been approached to skipper the *Darlwyne* but felt unwell and telephoned on the Sunday morning to withdraw from the trip.[10] Crucially, it was Robert Rainbird whom he telephoned rather than Brian Bown's family, a fact which further weakens Rainbird's denial of any involvement in the ill-fated voyage. Of course this begs the question, why would MacColl have been asked to skipper the *Darlwyne* when that was Brian Bown's role? It may be that two different people were trying to organise the same trip. We may never know for sure, but what we do know is that it seems likely that both Chard and MacColl may, like much of the rest of the country, have been suffering from the effects of the World Cup celebrations the previous night.

So with the die cast and 31 people poised to make a journey of some 23 nautical miles in a poorly maintained, overloaded and inherently unstable vessel with poor steering, the wrong engines, no safety equipment and rot in the hull, it seems only clear and calm conditions could offer them any hope of a safe passage. Tragically, as we shall see, those conditions were not forthcoming.

8. Author interview with holidaymaker who wished to remain anonymous.
9. *Falmouth Packet*, 23rd December 1966.
10. *The Mysterious Loss of the Darlwyne: A Cornish Holiday Tragedy*, Martin Banks, Tamar Books. 2014.

‘The man who has experienced shipwreck shudders even at a calm sea.’

Ovid

CHAPTER 3

Prelude to Disaster

On the morning of Sunday the 31st of July 1966, the sun crossed the horizon at 05.47 BST, an hour after low water at Falmouth. The tide was a gentle neap with a range of just three metres. With high water at 10.45 and the next low at 17.19, the *Darlwyne* would be motoring against the tidal stream on both legs of the passage, but a neap tide such as this would barely affect her apart from generating the usual eddies over the Bizzies reef in Veryan Bay, and the Field and Bellows reefs off Dodman Point, all of which she would pass close by en route.

The weather forecast was not ideal. Fresh to strong west to northwest winds, force five to seven (18–38mph) and veering to the southwest later. The weather during the last week of July was dominated by a low pressure system centred to the southeast of Iceland which brought squalls and rain to most of the country. The Meteorological Office summary from the Isles of Scilly reported rain from 12.25 onwards and the wind increasing from a force four to a force seven coming from the west. In other words, a storm was brewing just 70 miles away and it was heading for the south coast of Cornwall. But the unfavourable forecast did nothing to deter Brian Bown; in fact we do not know whether he even bothered to listen to it.

The weather was fairly sunny, but there was a significant breeze when the passengers assembled at Greatwood quay, ready to embark. It was at this point that the first problem of the day became apparent. The perennial steering issue afflicting the *Darlwyne* once again reared its ugly head with the result that Bown was unable to bring the boat alongside at the quay. It is worth noting that the base of Greatwood quay is surrounded by a steep rocky bank, which would only have added to the difficulty in coming alongside. Nevertheless, the steering issue was certainly the major contributor to Bown's decision to anchor just offshore. The passengers were then rowed out to the *Darlwyne* from the beach next to Greatwood quay in one of the two smaller boats that were either towed behind her or mounted on the davits at the stern, a process which took about half-an-hour. The larger of the two boats, a 16-foot Norwegian skiff actually belonged to Robert Rainbird's son. Since two boats were used, it seems likely that Rainbird was involved with the process of embarking the passengers. He was certainly present as he later told the *Daily Express*: 'They were the usual jolly crowd, laughing and joking.' His wife Gertrude was also there to see the guests off. 'The boat looked so pretty', she said.[1] With the passengers and plenty of food and drink on board, the *Darlwyne* cast off and set a course to the south, along the great natural harbour of the Fal Estuary known as the Carrick Roads. After some three nautical miles they rounded the lighthouse at St Anthony's Head and at nearby Zone Point turned to a northeasterly course towards Fowey.

There is some contention about the course that was taken. Some sources suggest that a detour was made so that the passengers could view the harbour at Mevagissey, about seven nautical miles from Fowey. This may indeed have happened; however it would have meant a total detour of some six-and-a-half nautical miles from the original course with the associated time and fuel consumption issues. In addition to this there would have been some practical problems. Mevagissey harbour is divided into an inner and an outer harbour. The inner harbour is the more picturesque of the two and is surrounded by gift shops and restaurants. It is however a working harbour and pleasure craft are not normally permitted to use it. In addition, it is very tidal and dries when the tide drops, which would have been the case at the time of the alleged visit. Whilst the outer harbour

1. *Daily Express*, 2nd August 1966.

would have been accessible, it has quite a narrow entrance and contains a large number of moored boats. For a vessel with such poor manoeuvring capabilities as the *Darlwyne*, Mevagissey outer harbour would have proved challenging and, given that from sea level little of the town is actually visible, I have considerable doubts that this detour actually took place.

What is known is that by 13.00, the *Darlwyne* had reached Fowey. By now it was raining hard and the breeze was quite fresh, but this seems not to have dampened the spirits of the passengers who were looking forward to spending the afternoon in the picturesque town. Once again, the steering problem became evident and the vessel anchored some distance from Albert Quay and once more the passengers were transported ashore by dinghy in three waves. Local fisherman John McDonald saw this and was concerned that the small boat seemed overloaded. He suggested to Brian Bown that it would be more sensible to bring the *Darlwyne* alongside the quay. He reported that Bown's reply was: 'Can't do that, she's a bitch to handle'.[2]

Once ashore, the passengers spent some three hours exploring the picturesque harbour-side shops and cafés, despite the fact that the weather was now pretty dreadful with a force six wind and heavy rain. A local restaurant proprietor called Ernest Billingsbury watched the party re-join their vessel and was concerned that, once more, the dinghy seemed to be so overloaded as to be 'down to the gunwales'. Billingsbury later stated that he heard a local fisherman called Johnny Richards warn Brian Bown against heading out into the gathering storm. Richards shouted: 'Go to Polruan across the bay and anchor up until the moon comes up at midnight.' Brian Bown's response was succinct. He shouted back: 'Mind your own business!'[3]

The Polruan Coastguard Station recorded the *Darlwyne* leaving Fowey at 16.45. A child (possibly Joel Hicks) was visible playing with a toy windmill. As the boat left the estuary she was sighted by a local boatman called Ernest Holder, who had been fishing from his boat close to the

2. *Daily Express*, 2nd August 1966.
3. *Daily Express*, 2nd August 1966.

Cannis South Cardinal buoy which is positioned about half a nautical mile southeast of Gribben Head. By now the wind had reached force seven and Holder was preparing to make a run for the shelter of Fowey. He reported that: 'She passed within about 30 yards of us. Just as they went by I caught a big fish and all the passengers on the Darlwin [sic] waved and shouted. The last I saw of her was when she was motoring off to the west'.[4] Nobody on board would be seen alive again.

There has been much conjecture concerning what happened between the time that the *Darlwyne* left Fowey and the time that she foundered, and we will never know for certain. What we can be sure of is that she sank around 21.00 as this was the time at which the watches of the recovered bodies were stopped. So, assuming that she didn't sink as soon as she left Fowey, there are about four hours that remain a complete mystery.

One theory certainly has some merit and is worth examining more closely. Martin Banks has suggested that the *Darlwyne* may have struggled some distance across Veryan Bay until a mutiny occurred, forcing the vessel to turn around and thereby exposing her vulnerable stern to the full force of the storm.[5] Whilst Brian Bown had a degree of seafaring experience, Ray Mills and Albert Russel were experienced sailors too and Kenneth Robinson and John Russel were professional Merchant Navy officers. It is clear that the party knew they were in trouble because Jean Brock was wearing her husband's wedding ring and jumper. Did one or more of the experienced sailors on board take over the helm and attempt to run for shelter on the east side of Dodman Point? We shall never know but it is an intriguing possibility.[6]

It may also be that the *Darlwyne* was simply struggling, unable to make much headway as she was overloaded and in heavy seas. Perhaps she had engine trouble. Again it's all theoretical but no less interesting for that.

There are a number of alleged sightings and it's worth examining them carefully. The first of these was by two men who were fishing from a boat

4. *Daily Express*, 2nd August 1966.
5. Martin Banks is an actor and theatre director who developed an interest in the Darlwyne and wrote a book, *The Mysterious Loss of The Darlwyne*, (2014, Tamar Books).
6. Author interview with Martin Banks.

just off Gorran Haven. They claimed to have seen the *Darlwyne* passing them on a southwesterly course and it's quite likely that they did. Then, at about 17.45, a farmer called Leslie Smith was working in his field on the west side of the Dodman when he claimed to have seen a boat matching the description of the *Darlwyne* near Hemmick Beach on a course for Gull Rock. He said there were about a dozen people standing on the after deck. He said it had a single word name on the transom but at that distance he couldn't read it. Was this boat the *Darlwyne*? Again, it could have been, but there are some issues with this account. Firstly, if a dozen people were on the after deck and Brian Bown was at the wheel, where were the other 18 people on board? Some may have been in the wheelhouse but 18 would be quite a squeeze in a space eight feet square. Then there is the position of the boat. Hemmick Beach is tucked away in the northeastern corner of Veryan Bay, close to Dodman Point. It is not where a vessel would be if it was on a course from the Dodman to Gull Rock, near Nare Head; in fact it is 90 degrees off course. Smith also stated that he couldn't see if the vessel in question was towing another boat. This seems rather odd because he could count, at least roughly, the number of people on deck but couldn't see a 16-foot skiff. There is no suggestion that any of them were being dishonest, but these issues simply serve to highlight the difficulties with eyewitness accounts.

The last reported sighting of the *Darlwyne* was by a Mrs Fuller of Portloe. She stated that she was with her young daughter, looking out to sea with her binoculars when she saw a boat that she later thought could have been the *Darlwyne*, about two thirds of the way across Veryan Bay and heading for Gull Rock. She went to get her daughter a shawl and when she returned the boat was out of sight. The position she gave would have put the boat some three nautical miles from where she was standing. It seems inconceivable that a boat which was some three miles away could be identified in calm weather, let alone torrential rain and spray. Mrs Fuller also said that the boat she saw was blue, but the *Darlwyne* was white.

Another altogether different report was received by the police that evening. A tourist reported seeing four people clinging to Diamond Rock on the eastern side of Porthluney Cove, near Caerhays Castle. The information was given to the Caerhays Estate manager, a Mr J H Trudgeon. Sergeant Harris from Tregony Police Station who took the report speculated that there was a possibility that these people may have been victims of the *Darlwyne*.[7] This is highly unlikely for reasons that we shall examine later, but it certainly adds intrigue to an already fascinating story. In the meantime, one thing is certain. Somewhere out there in a hellish maelstrom, the passengers of the *Darlwyne* were fighting for their very lives.

7. *Falmouth Packet*, 23rd December 1966.

'The Westerly Wind asserting his sway from the south-west quarter is often like a monarch gone mad, driving forth with wild imprecations the most faithful of his courtiers to shipwreck, disaster, and death.'

Joseph Conrad

CHAPTER 4

'When is Daddy coming back?'

At the Greatwood Hotel, just five people remained and, but for the swaying tree tops and the persistent rain, they were unaware of the dreadful conditions at sea. Robert and Gertrude Rainbird, Beryl Mills and her youngest child Lisa, and Megan Hicks still had no reason to doubt that the *Darlwyne* would return to the quay on schedule. The tables in the dining room were laid and the evening meal was being cooked ready for a 19.00 sitting. In Penryn, John Barratt's wife was the first to notice that the *Darlwyne* had not returned to her usual mooring. She voiced her concern to Christopher Mitchell, her son-in-law, who decided to telephone Greatwood to see if the boat had disembarked its passengers yet. Robert Rainbird told him that the *Darlwyne* had not yet returned. Mitchell then went to Falmouth Coastguard Station, arriving at 19.27.[1]

On duty that evening was Coastguard Ernest Edward Seager. Mitchell asked Seager if a log of any yacht's movements in and out of Falmouth had been recorded. Seager told him that the sheer volume of small boat traffic would have made that impossible. Nevertheless, he checked the log of shipping movements, but the *Darlwyne* was not listed on it. Seager later claimed that Mitchell expressed no urgency or anxiety about the vessel. He advised him to see if the *Darlwyne* had actually left Fowey.

1. Report of Court No. 8042 M.V. Darlwyne.

Unfortunately, Ernest Seager did not make any record of this conversation as he considered it to be a casual enquiry.

Christopher Mitchell returned home and telephoned various friends and acquaintances in the Helford Estuary area and elsewhere to determine if they had sighted the *Darlwyne*. Nobody had done so. At 21.35, Robert Rainbird telephoned Falmouth coastguard and spoke to coastguard Seager (Rainbird later claimed that this call took place earlier, at 20.00). Seager recognized that this was the same vessel that Mitchell had enquired about two hours previously. He advised Rainbird to telephone a number of other coastguard stations and report back to him with his findings. Inexplicably, Seager seems not to have foreseen a potential emergency at this stage. Robert Rainbird telephoned the coastguard stations at Polruan, Gorran Haven and Mevagissey. Polruan coastguard informed him that the *Darlwyne* had left Fowey at 16.45. Rainbird then claimed to have telephoned Falmouth coastguard at 22.15 with this information, but Seager denied receiving this call and was relieved from his watch at 23.00 without recording it. This small anomaly is crucial. If the call was made and disregarded, then Seager certainly risked being held to be negligent in not raising the alarm, but if not, then no blame can be apportioned for any delay in the subsequent search.

What is certain is that at 02.45 on Monday the 1st of August, Robert Rainbird again telephoned Falmouth coastguard and spoke to Brian Beard, who was Seager's relief officer. Rainbird had already contacted the harbour masters at Mevagissey, Par, and Charlestown with no news forthcoming. Coastguard Beard knew nothing about the previous enquiries regarding the *Darlwyne* and immediately alerted his district officer who initiated a major search to begin at daybreak.[2]

At 05.34, Falmouth coastguard began to broadcast an emergency message to all craft within its jurisdiction. At 05.37, the Falmouth Lifeboat was launched, followed by the Fowey Lifeboat some 18 minutes later. By 06.45, the first helicopters from RAF Chivenor were searching the coast between Falmouth and Fowey to a range of five nautical miles out to sea.

2. Report of Court No. 8042 M.V. Darlwyne.

Just 15 minutes later, that search area was extended offshore by another three nautical miles and as far east as Plymouth. By 09.45, Shackleton aircraft from RAF St Mawgan were in the air and searching a massive area from the Lizard Peninsula in the west to Prawle Point near Salcombe in Devon to the east, and as far south as the 49th parallel which cuts across the Bay of Biscay. Soon, the Royal Navy had its ships as well as its helicopters involved. HMS *Fearless*, a newly commissioned amphibious assault ship arrived to search offshore of Dodman Point. The aircraft carrier, HMS *Ark Royal* was heading out of Devonport en route for Portsmouth when she was diverted to help with the search. How much urgency was given to the task is open to speculation. I spoke to one crew member of *Ark Royal* who was on board that day who told me that he was unaware that a search was taking place at all.[3]

More Royal Navy ships joined the search, with the frigate HMS *Phoebe* and the survey ship HMS *Hecate* being directed by one of the Shackleton aircraft.

With the coastguard conducting an extensive search of the shoreline, the first discovery of note was actually made some way out to sea when a crew member of the passing 1100-ton coastal oil tanker, *Esso Caernarvon* spotted the 16-foot skiff which was towed behind the *Darlwyne*, some 20 nautical miles from Dodman Point, bearing 302 degrees, which put it at about nine miles from the Eddystone Lighthouse. The Royal Navy sent a helicopter to the location and a winchman was lowered aboard. He found empty fuel containers, a lifejacket, and the oars in place. The painter had been cut. The skiff was towed to Falmouth by an RAF launch. Among those on board was Robert Rainbird.

It was at this point that some deck planking was found and with it, a red and white lifebelt bearing the name 'Lady Beatrice'. This was known to have been carried aboard the *Darlwyne*. The *Lady Beatrice* was a boat previously owned either by John Barratt or his son.

It was clear that a major news story was unfolding, though at this time there was still an expectation that the *Darlwyne* would be found afloat

3. Author interview with contemporary member of HMS *Ark Royal* crew.

with its passengers alive. Even without the benefit of today's communications technology, the agonizing wait for news was reported globally and with varying degrees of accuracy. One newspaper in Canada confidently asserted that the *Darlwyne* had been blown offshore but had plenty of provisions on board. For those closer to home, the reality was more sombre, but hope was not yet lost. The media circus focused its attention primarily on Greatwood.

The *Falmouth Packet* newspaper is published weekly, so the story describing the scene at Greatwood on Monday the 1st of August was actually published on Friday the 5th and it makes grim reading. The reporter was David Mudd, who was to become the Member of Parliament for Falmouth and Camborne in 1970. The police had moved swiftly to close the narrow lane leading down to Greatwood to everyone except the local doctor and vicar, in order to give some privacy to those who were waiting for news. In his book, *The Cruel Cornish Sea*, he wrote:

> 'The morning of 1 August 1966 was one of those glorious summer days. As I drove towards Mylor I was not unduly worried. I was on my way to a story that would, I felt sure, have a speedy and happy ending and would turn out to have been nothing more than a combination of misunderstanding and groundless fears'.[4]

Apparently, Mudd was able to talk his way through the road block and report on the heartbreaking scene at the hotel. He describes what he called an atmosphere of 'suspended life'. He went on:

> 'From upstairs windows the inevitable display of bathing gear and towels fluttered with the merry signal of holiday gaiety. A car parked outside still had the confetti of a honeymoon couple. Makeshift cricket stumps, a tennis ball and a discarded sandal showed where children had, impatiently, had an impromptu game while waiting to be taken on the trip'.

4. *The Cruel Cornish Sea* by David Mudd. Bossiney Books, 1981.

Most heart-breaking of all, David Mudd describes coming across three-year-old Lisa Mills playing alone and repeatedly asking her mother, 'When is Daddy coming back?'

Having already lost her first husband in similar circumstances, we can scarcely imagine what was going on in the mind of Megan Hicks. She told the *Daily Express*: 'It has been an absolute nightmare. I did a lot of work in the hotel today to try and keep my mind busy'.[5] The Vicar of Mylor, the Reverend Frank Martin, maintained a constant vigil at Greatwood. He spoke admiringly of Beryl Mills to the *Falmouth Packet*: 'Mrs Mills struck me as being a woman of great character who is really being magnificent. As hope fades she is showing great courage'.[6]

Hope may well have been fading but it had not run out completely. The nuns who ran the convent school attended by Susan and Nicola Tassell held a prayer vigil for their safe return. Elsewhere, more practical measures were being taken and the search at sea continued. On Tuesday the 2nd of August, thick fog hampered the air search, but the lifeboats continued to look. Jim Turpin, coxswain of the Fowey Lifeboat told *The Sun* newspaper: 'We have been searching for 15 hours and found nothing. It is a mystery. The Darlwin [sic] has absolutely disappeared. I have never seen the bay so clean of wreckage. There was not a thing to suggest that a boat had been wrecked out there'.[7] Robert Rainbird stated his opinion that the *Darlwyne* may still be afloat, albeit out of fuel and drifting towards the Channel Islands. In fact, she was fitted with two 30-gallon fuel tanks which would have allowed for about 15 hours of running at two thirds power, so the fuel would likely have run out considerably earlier.

Various items were retrieved from the sea by the search boats including a small white rudder from a dinghy and several buckets, but they were ruled out as having come from the *Darlwyne*. A patch of oil ten miles east of Coverack on the Lizard Peninsula was similarly dismissed. In Devon, the Salcombe Lifeboat recovered a length of blue plastic, some marine plywood and a jerry can which were also ruled out as evidence.

5. *Daily Express*, 2nd August 1966.
6. *Falmouth Packet*, 5th August 1966.
7. *The Sun*, 3rd August 1966.

Later that day James Giles arrived at Greatwood. He was a colleague of Raymond Mills and had concerns about the search which he shared with Donald Bartholomew, the chairman of the company they both worked for. Bartholomew chartered three Dragon Rapide aircraft from Lands End Airport to conduct a search further south in the Bay of Biscay and further east to include the Channel Islands. He told the *Daily Mail*: 'Beryl Mills, Raymond's wife, will not believe all hope has gone until evidence is produced.' The Rapides searched an astonishing 14,000 square miles of sea between them at a cost of £1,330, but found no trace of the *Darlwyne*. After refuelling in Jersey, they flew back to Lands End the following day, just as the first bodies were being discovered.

Along with the bodies of Albert and Margaret Russel, Susan Tassell and Amanda Hicks, the search team found a few pieces of wreckage. There was some hull planking of double diagonal construction, an engine cover, a child's plastic football and a tin of sun lotion. Both the Falmouth and Fowey lifeboats headed for Falmouth with their grim cargoes. It later transpired that the Falmouth Lifeboat had spotted a fifth body, that of a man on the surface, but as they approached, it sank out of reach. We will never know who this person was, if he subsequently washed up, or if he disappeared forever.

The whole town was paralysed with grief. Shopkeepers drew their blinds, crowds stood, heads bowed in respectful silence as the coffins were landed on the quayside. Just offshore, the Royal Yacht *Britannia* was anchored and dressed with bunting to celebrate the Queen Mother's 66th birthday. Before the lifeboats passed, the bunting was removed, and the ensign was flown at half-mast.

On the 7th of August, with Jean Brock's body having also been found, a service was conducted on Custom House Quay in Falmouth by the Rector of Falmouth, Cannon T Barfett, to commemorate what were now certainly the 31 dead of the *Darlwyne*. The following day, as the bodies of Margaret Wright and Susan Cowan were being brought ashore, Amanda Hicks was buried in the churchyard at Mylor. Thirty-eight years later she would be joined by her mother, Megan. Her brother Joel was never found and is commemorated on the gravestone as 'lost at sea'.

A Movietone newsreel shot as the story was unfolding, captured some of the atmosphere. Sombre images of the coffins coming ashore at Falmouth were accompanied by mournful music. There is rare footage, too, of Robert Rainbird (in the commentary by veteran announcer Leslie Mitchell, he is mistakenly called Richard Rainbird) walking his dog beside Greatwood Beach. The final scene is of Greatwood with the abandoned cars and swimsuits still drying in the sun.[8]

Some people were already sure that they knew what had happened. Steven Gifford, who had bought the *Darlwyne* from John Barratt, only to have it repossessed, gave a forthright newspaper interview, possibly seeing a chance to discredit Barratt.

> 'To have put 31 people aboard that boat on a voyage of that length was ridiculous. I couldn't sleep all night thinking about those poor people in a boat that at one time had no watertight bulkhead, was riddled with rot and woodworm and had been holed in so many places. I found that the walls in the front saloon were lined with three-ply. On removing planks from the port side I saw extensive rot which could be taken out by the handful… I'm certain that what happened was that the boat was not in sound enough condition to have been pounded by heavy seas and it must have broken up or sank quickly so that the people on board did not have time to reach the dinghies'.[9]

Of course, even in the presence of terrible grief, there are practical problems to deal with. For example, all the cars of the victims were essentially stranded at Greatwood. Falmouth Round Table organized a group of drivers to return them to the families all over the country. The families who were able to travel made their way to Mylor to retrieve the other possessions. Particularly poignant was the discovery by Peter Tassell's parents of his lucky Victorian Crown coin which he always carried with him, but which he had left behind on this occasion. As his father remarked: 'That was the day Peter's luck ran out.'[10] Many of the victims' clothes,

8. This is now freely available on www.aparchive.com — search for 'Disaster of the Darlwin'.
9. *The Daily Sketch*, 3rd August 1966.
10. *Falmouth Packet*, 16th December 1966.

particularly those of the children, were left behind. They were collected by a team of Women's Voluntary Service (WVS) volunteers, led by Mrs D Insley. They distributed them to the Pestalozzi Village in Sussex, which was a centre dedicated to looking after refugee children, and to a region of Turkey which had suffered an earthquake.

Identifying a body, particularly when it has been retrieved from the sea, is a deeply unpleasant task as I know from personal experience, but it is a legal requirement before an inquest can be opened or a death certificate issued. Megan Hicks was saved the trauma of this task as Amanda was identified by her uncle, Peter Badcock. Susan Tassell was identified by her godmother; Eileen Tassell by her brother-in-law, William Hudson. Ray Mills was identified by James Giles, who had organized the private air search. Due to the length of time that Mills had been in the water, Giles identified him by recognizing his distinctive Omega watch and a key fob in his anorak pocket bearing the name of his employers, Johnson and Co of Liverpool. Susan Cowan and Margaret Wright were identified by their uncle, Norman Tyer. Patricia Russel and Janice Mills were identified by Arnold Moxon. Most admirably of all, despite her overwhelming grief, Beryl Mills volunteered to identify Albert and Margaret Russel. Given that all the bodies were already badly decomposed, these people are to be praised for their fortitude.

Many of the victims, including the Mills and Tassell family were cremated at the Penmount Crematorium just outside Truro, and their ashes were returned home to their families.

On the 3rd of September, the Falmouth Lifeboat, *Crawford and Constance Coneybeare* with coxswain Bert West at the helm, slipped out of Falmouth Harbour. On board were the Reverend Frank Martin and five members of the Tassell family. The boat hove to a few miles from Dodman Point and four wreaths and the ashes of Susan and Eileen were scattered on the sea.

At the village school in Mylor, a special assembly was led by the headmaster, Mr Piper. Dene Berryman (née Smith) recalled: 'It was a terribly sad day. Joel's (Hicks) desk was empty, I'll never forget that. We were very young, and it was our first experience of death.'[11]

With the recovered victims now at rest, questions needed to be answered. Where were the other 19 bodies? Where was the wreck of the *Darlwyne*? And why did she sink?

11. Author interview with Dene Berryman (née Smith).

‘I have come to the conclusion that politics are too serious a matter to be left to the politicians.’

Charles de Gaulle

CHAPTER 5

Questions on Land and Sea

In Parliament on the 2nd of August 1966, The President of the Board of Trade, Douglas Jay, announced a preliminary enquiry into the disappearance of the *Darlwyne*.[1] Even before the first bodies had appeared, questions were being asked in the House. His decision was prompted by the MP for Truro, Geoffrey Wilson, who had asked about the *Darlwyne* in particular, and the regulations for commercial vessels in general.

The following day, *The Times* published an editorial entitled 'Where An Enquiry is Needed', backing Jay's decision and highlighting the lack of enforcement of the Merchant Shipping Act of 1894. It ended the piece with a stark statement:

> 'Whatever happened to the Darlwin [sic] — that is still unknown — there is a general lesson to be hammered home with every marine accident. The sea must be respected and to some extent feared. Without that awareness, tragedy is always near.'[2]

The responsibility for the preliminary enquiry fell to Norman Bramald, a senior Board of Trade inspector. His job was to gather evidence 'sifting

1. *The Times*, 3rd August 1966.
2. Ibid.

fact from rumour and getting as true a picture of the tragedy as possible.'[3] Bramald was already asking questions about Robert Rainbird's version of events relating to his contact with the coastguard on the night of the 31st. In Parliament too, prior to the discovery of any evidence that the *Darlwyne* had sunk, the matter of the way in which the search was initiated was the subject of some concern.

Peter Bessel, MP for Bodmin took the opportunity to question Merlyn Rees MP, Under Secretary of State for Defence whose remit included the RAF. Bessel was scathing in his criticism:

> 'I suggest that this is a matter of very considerable urgency. I suggest that there has been a totally inadequate rescue attempt made by the departments concerned and responsible. I suggest that it is vital that the search be extended to take in a much larger area of the sea ... It has been suggested to me that it is quite possible that in the time that had elapsed this ship could have floated or sailed away as far as the Bay of Biscay. There is no evidence of wreckage. No boats have been recovered. There is no reason to suppose this boat has sunk. It is a boat of strong construction, and I am assured, again by expert opinion, that it is very unlikely she would founder even in heavy seas, and even though very badly overloaded ... what I am concerned about ... is the degree of effort being made by the Defence Ministry, by the Board of Trade and by every responsible person to see that the maximum possible effort is being made ... The lives of 31 people are at stake. It is quite possible — although I admit, doubtful — that those people are still alive. I believe the whole House will demand a searching enquiry into this matter. It is not enough to have a smooth ministerial answer. We want assurance that everything humanly possible will now be undertaken, for at this moment the relatives are so concerned that they are actually hiring private aircraft to carry out a job that should be carried out by the Royal Air Force.'[4]

Merlyn Rees was having none of it. He was a rising political star, who was later to serve as Home Secretary in the mid-1970s and go on to the

---

3. *Falmouth Packet*, 5th August 1966.
4. Hansard, 3rd August 1966.

House of Lords as a life peer. His response was forthright and unequivocal:

'I regret, given the serious nature of the accident that has taken place this week and which has touched the hearts of many people in this country, that the Honourable Member for Bodmin should seek to refer to it in the manner which he has just done ... I should now like to give the facts as I have had them ... The coastguards alerted the Royal Air Force through the usual channels at 06.00 hours on Monday, and from that time onwards four sorties were carried out by helicopters from Chivenor. At 8 o'clock, a Shackleton took off from St Mawgan. I make it clear that the crews of the Shackletons at St Mawgan are properly trained for square searches in the western approaches ... I have been advised that one aircraft from these squadrons was sufficient to do the job. This was Monday from 8am to 8pm ... On Tuesday morning a Shackleton took off at 8 o'clock but ceased searching at mid-day. I am also very firmly advised that because of the force eight gale, because of the very, very bad visibility, it was impossible to carry out the search ... the helicopters also gave the same advice ... I would also point out the nature of the sea at such a time makes it extremely difficult, whatever the visibility is, to see what is going on in the water ... There was no lack of urgency and regret the implication that has been made ... I regret what the Honourable Gentleman has said about the lack of urgency. That is not the case. We shall go on searching ... This is the work of the coastguards and lifeboats as well. Everything possible has been done, and it is grossly unfair to the relatives of these people to suggest that there is any dereliction of duty at this time.'[5]

Robert Rainbird had contacted Geoffrey Wilson, MP for Truro, who made a more conciliatory statement to the House:

'I do not want to associate myself with any criticism of the RAF, but I heard from Mr Rainbird, the proprietor of the hotel from which most of these people came ... He told me that he knew this boat well and that it had lifeboats and other moveable material on the deck. He raised the question whether it could have sunk without some trace being found. He thought it might have drifted towards

5. Hansard, 3rd August 1966.

the Bay of Biscay. I enquired from the Board of Trade … and was told the RAF had searched … a very considerable area and beyond which the vessel would have drifted. I hope the search will be continued in case there is any possibility that it has gone in the Biscay direction as Mr Rainbird thinks.'[6]

Two days later, on the 5th of August, Merlyn Rees rose to make a statement to the House:

… at 6.22am a Shackleton located wreckage and two bodies in the search area southeast of Dodman Point, which is virtually the datum point on which the search was based. Two further bodies in the same area were located by an RN helicopter. The four bodies and lifebelt were subsequently brought to Falmouth by RNLI lifeboats. Some of these have now been positively identified as having been passengers of the Darlwin [sic]… The wreckage found yesterday came to the surface in the middle of the initial search area. I hope this will be accepted as vindicating the judgement of the experts who determined what this area should be. The search is still going on under the direction of the RAF rescue co-ordination centre in Plymouth as it has since the search began. I am sure the House will wish me to pay tribute to the Navy, the RAF, the Coastguards, the Lifeboat Service and all those who have helped in any way in this operation. Once more I want to express also the sympathy of the House to relatives and friends of the victims of this tragedy.'[7]

Peter Bessel was determined to continue his spat with Merlyn Rees, though it's hard to see what he hoped to gain from it apart from political point scoring. He asked:

'May I ask the Honourable Gentleman whether he accepts the facts which I gave to the House, as they were supplied to me, by his Right Honourable Friend the President of the Board of Trade, on Wednesday were substantially correct?'[8]

---

6. Hansard, 3rd August 1966.
7. Hansard, 5th August 1966.
8. Hansard, 5th August 1966.

Merlyn Rees gave a frosty reply to the question:

'No Sir. I have inquired into this very carefully, even in the last hour. The Honourable Gentleman quite correctly telephoned the private office of my Honourable Friend. There are two aspects of this. First of all, with regard to the information which the Honourable Gentleman gave in the House concerning what happened on Monday, which I denied in the House on Wednesday, it is denied absolutely that these facts were given to the Honourable Gentleman. With regard to the Wednesday aspect of things, the Honourable Gentleman telephoned the private office and it telephoned the private office of my Noble Friend, the Minister. The office's instructions are to be as helpful as possible, and it gave the Honourable Gentleman information as it was happening. I have looked at the television broadcast in which the Honourable Gentleman took part last evening, and all I can say in this brief moment is that he has misunderstood what was happening at the time …'[9]

Peter Bessel was determined to pursue his agenda and responded:

'In view of the Honourable Gentleman's statement, may I affirm again, without equivocation whatever, that the information which I gave to the House about the events on Monday was that which was supplied to me by the private office of his Right Honourable Friend the President of the Board of Trade? I have a witness to this conversation. Furthermore, does the Honourable Gentleman agree that the facts as I gave them to the House relating to the subsequent events on Tuesday and Wednesday morning were correct?'[10]

Again, Merlyn Rees stood his ground and replied with a rebuke:

'I repeat again that there can be no question of what happened on Monday, because I gave the facts of the matter to the House two days ago. I am only sorry that last night, I am given to understand, the Honourable Gentleman used the

9. Hansard, 5th August 1966.
10. Hansard, 5th August 1966.

> earlier information yet again. It is very difficult to deal with particular points across the floor of the House at the moment, but I dealt with the circumstances of Tuesday and Wednesday on Wednesday, and I am quite satisfied that everything possible was done to deal with this case. I understand that it has been suggested that the RAF took off only because private aircraft were taking off. That is not true. Statements of that kind only do a great deal of harm to the morale of a very great group of servicemen and RNLI and coastguard men who have been working extremely hard for the last week.'[11]

Outside of the sanitized atmosphere of the House of Commons, there was altogether more unpleasant but equally important work to be done. All of the bodies had to have post mortem examinations conducted on them. All were in varying states of decomposition. The examinations were carried out by the Devon County pathologist, Dr Frederick Hocking. He was particularly experienced in this type of examination, having conducted over 600 post mortems on drowning victims. He concluded that none of the bodies had fractured bones, which ruled out an explosion having taken place. He further determined that all the victims had been 'deep drowned': in other words they had been dragged deep underwater rather than struggling on the surface. This even applied to Jean Brock, despite the fact that she was wearing a lifebelt. But the lifebelt did not conform to the standard required by the Board of Trade as, at 24 inches in diameter instead of the regulation 30 inches, it had insufficient buoyancy. It was also noted that she was wearing a man's jumper, probably her husband's, and a wedding ring that was certainly his, suggesting that those on board were aware that they were in serious trouble at some point before the *Darlwyne* sank.

Of particular significance were the watches that some of the victims were wearing, as the time that they stopped would give an indication of the time that the *Darlwyne* sank. They were as follows:

> A waterproof, self-winding watch which was still going (belonging to Ray Mills).

11. Hansard, 5th August 1966.

A watch which had stopped at 8.05 but which was run down and when wound up started again (belonging to Albert Russel).

A lady's watch which stopped at 9.20 (belonging to Amanda Hicks).

A lady's watch which stopped at 9.17. (belonging to Margaret Wright).

A child's watch which stopped at 9.19 (possibly belonging to Janice Mills).

A lady's watch which stopped at 9.49.

The watches were tested to determine how long they would have to be immersed before they stopped. The watch which stopped at 9.19 would stop after ten minutes and the watch which stopped at 9.49 would take an hour to stop.[12]

With what little information that could be obtained from the bodies duly recorded, the central question still needed to be answered; where was the *Darlwyne*? That problem fell to the Royal Navy to solve. With the Cold War in full swing, the navy had been allocated a generous budget in order to remain a credible deterrent to the Soviet threat, and some of that money had been put into the development of mine hunting technology. There had been massive improvement since the first Anti-Submarine Detection Investigation Committee (ASDIC) underwater/sonar system used in the Second World War. The 'Ton' class of mine hunters were fitted with such sensitive equipment that HMS *Shoulton* was said to have detected a wedding ring on the seabed which had been dropped off the jetty in one of her ports of call. HMS *Iveston* was similarly equipped and in early December of 1966, she began a systematic search of Veryan Bay from Gull Rock to a point just west of the Dodman.

HMS *Iveston* was a 360-ton minehunter which later gained notoriety as the last ship in the Royal Navy to experience a mutiny. In 1970 at Ullapool, five members of the crew barricaded the door to the officer's mess after a

12. Report of Court No. 8042 M.V. Darlwyne.

heavy drinking session and subjected their captives to a lengthy concert of Irish republican songs. They were jailed and dismissed from the service. In 1966, however, the crew were a disciplined and well-trained unit and determined to find some trace of the *Darlwyne*. Some of the detection equipment on board was so new, and so secret, that specialists from the companies which manufactured it were brought in to assist.

Over a period of 27 days, HMS *Iveston* made no fewer than 3,500 contacts in Veryan Bay with a team of 15 divers making more than 600 dives to investigate the most likely ones. In charge of the search was Lieutenant Commander Jim Dale, himself a Cornishman, who had previously taken charge of the salvage of a crashed Buccaneer aircraft off the Lizard which was the deepest working dive ever undertaken in the world up to that point.

HMS *Iveston* was based in Rosyth and her divers were hand-picked from Plymouth Command Deep Diving Team and clearance divers from HMS *Vernon* in Portsmouth. She had been working on a salvage operation in Portland alongside the salvage support vessel Pintail which also accompanied her to Cornwall. The divers used both traditional standard dress and scuba equipment to depths of 200 feet (61 metres). A total of 15 square miles of seabed was meticulously searched, often in appalling weather. No trace of the *Darlwyne* was found. The commanding officer of HMS *Iveston*, Lieutenant Commander Arthur Ginn, received a signal from Vice Admiral Sir Fitzroy Talbot praising the team's efforts. It read:

> 'I have been most impressed by the way you and the Plymouth Command deep divers have carried out the Darlwin [sic] search operation under difficult conditions. I am sorry that in the limited time available luck has not been on your side to give you the success you well deserve.'[13]

This, however was not quite the end of the search. On Friday the 13th of January 1967, the Royal Navy were again asked to take part. A fisherman had reported that his net had been snagged by a submerged object that

13. *Falmouth Packet*, 4th November 1966.

was not marked on any navigational chart, five miles south-southeast of Gribben Head, latitude 50 degrees, 15 minutes, 32 seconds north, longitude 4 degrees, 37 minutes, 32 seconds west. This put it due east of Gorran Haven, due south of Polruan and some three miles northeast of where the first four bodies were discovered.[14]

Michael Thomas, spokesman for the Board of Trade, voiced doubts about the practicality of undertaking a 180-foot (55 metre) dive in winter conditions. He also questioned whether much useful information could be gathered, although he mentioned that if the engines were found to be partially dismantled, engine failure must be suspected. Again, no trace of the *Darlwyne* was discovered. All told, the cost of the search exceeded £20,000 and was met by the Board of Trade.

The fact was that the *Darlwyne* had sunk without trace. The Board of Trade still demanded answers and a court of enquiry was to be held to find them.

14. *Falmouth Packet*, 23rd December 1966.

‘The dead cannot cry out for justice; it is a duty of the living to do so for them.’

Lois McMaster Bujold

CHAPTER 6

Two Guilty Men

In the winter of 1966–67, Cornwall's striking modern council offices in Truro were still under construction, so the venue for the Court of Inquiry into the *Darlwyne* disaster was to be Old County Hall, about a quarter of a mile away in Station Road. Built in 1890, this imposing monument to civic pride still stands today. Elegant and classically proportioned, it is the epitome of Victorian municipal architecture. A grade two listed building, it has now been converted into luxury apartments.

On Tuesday December the 13th 1966, the inquiry began with the remit of establishing the circumstances in which the *Darlwyne* had been lost, but it was to have major repercussions for the commercial boating sector nationally. Sadly, her sinking was not the only maritime disaster involving significant loss of life that year. On the 22nd of July a clinker-built open ferry boat called the *Prince of Wales* was carrying 42 passengers (six more than it was licensed for) of whom 15 were children, from Barmouth up the River Mawddach to Penmaenpool in Wales. Due to 'negligent handling', the 72-year-old skipper, Edward Llewellyn Jones, crashed the vessel into one of the supports of the Penmaenpool Bridge.[1] The boat sank in seconds and 15 people including four children were killed.

The President of the Board of Trade, Douglas Jay, had already signalled

1. Report of Court No. 8041, M.V. Prince of Wales.

his intention to tighten up the regulations relating to the certification of commercial pleasure craft. At the time, the Merchant Shipping Act of 1894 covered any vessel plying for trade which carried more than twelve passengers. Although not covered by the Act, vessels carrying fewer than twelve passengers could be subject to the requirements of local authorities under the Public Health Act of 1907. The 1894 Act had previously been amended so that the person who was carrying out the statutory survey of a particular vessel was also required to determine the competence of the skipper. There was clearly a problem here because there was nothing to stop a competent mariner turning up during the survey in lieu of a less competent owner.

My own father underwent just such a process to obtain a waterman's permit in Plymouth in 1963. His boat was actually dry on the slipway and, although he was able to prove his nautical competence, there was no check to see that he was who he claimed to be, or even that his boat could actually float. The system certainly needed an overhaul.

This subject was to be a recurring theme during the inquiry. For example, the Falmouth Harbour Master, Captain F H Edwards, stated his opinion that with the maximum fine for operating a commercial vessel without a licence being just £5 it was not any sort of deterrent.[2]

The inquiry was chaired by John Naisby QC. Since he was called to the Bar in 1947, he had specialised in maritime and shipping law. He held the position of Commissioner of Wrecks, a role which these days would fall to both the Maritime and Coastguard Agency (MCA) and the Receiver of Wreck. He was assisted by Captain H S Hewson and Dr Ewan Corlett MA, PhD, MRINA. The opening submission was by Michael Thomas for the Board of Trade who stated that:

> 'There was no doubt that the *Darlwyne*'s last voyage, a day cruise from Falmouth to Fowey, was undertaken in flagrant disregard of the laws drawn up to protect the safety of passengers at sea ... The person or persons who were responsible in fact or in law for the *Darlwyne*'s sailing must have been totally ignorant, or

2. *The Times*, 21st December 1966.

cynically indifferent of their legal obligations.'[3]

He went on to express, on behalf of the President of the Board of Trade, 'very great sympathy to all those who had suffered a bereavement as a result of this shipping casualty.'[4]

Thomas told the inquiry that the evidence that was available would fall into five categories.

The first stage would be concerned with the history of the *Darlwyne* to find out 'what kind of boat she was, what kind of boat she became as a result of alterations, and her condition and equipment at the time of her last voyage.'

The second stage would be 'considering the circumstances in which she came to be carrying passengers from Falmouth to Fowey, in short, how the trip came to be organized.'

The third stage would consist of 'observations made of the *Darlwyne* during her last voyage from Fowey to sea, the evidence of the wind and sea conditions and particulars of the persons who were on board her.'

The fourth stage would be to 'direct the court's attention to the search and rescue operations that were undertaken and also the circumstances in which they came to be initiated.'

The fifth and final stage would be the production of some evidence which might 'on the basis of probability, assist the court to arrive at some conclusion as to the probable cause of the loss of the vessel.'[5]

There then followed a statement from Captain William P Learmouth, a Board of Trade nautical surveyor from Falmouth, who outlined five possible causes for the loss of the *Darlwyne* that night.

The first was that she may have struck a mine, which he said in that location at that time was all but impossible. The second was that she may have struck a floating object, but he qualified this by stating that it would have taken a floating object of considerable size to sink the *Darlwyne*. It has to be said that this statement was made before the evidence about the

3. Report of Court No. 8042 M.V. Darlwyne.
4. Ibid.
5. *Falmouth Packet*, 16th December 1966.

Darlwyne's poor state of repair was heard. Thirdly, collision with another vessel, but none had been reported and there would have been much more wreckage in evidence. The fourth possibility could have been navigational error. Again, there would have been more wreckage had she struck a reef. The most likely reef would have been the Whelps to the south of Gull Rock over which there would have been less than a metre of water at 19.00 on the night of the sinking, but that area had been carefully searched. Lastly was the possibility of foundering due to the poor weather. It was inevitable that, in those conditions, water would have entered the cockpit, making the vessel unstable and leading her to capsize.[6]

Much of the subsequent information related in the inquiry has already been discussed in this book, but there were moments of confrontation which are very much part of the overall story. The inquiry itself was, at times, ill-tempered and dramatic. Even on the first day, Arthur Robinson, the father of Kenneth Robinson, stood up and demanded to be given John Barratt's full name and address. Mr Naisby calmly assured him that such information would be given when Barratt came to give evidence.[7] On the second day of the inquiry, Robinson applied to be made a party to the proceedings so that he could ask his own questions, and this was granted, however on the 16th of December he withdrew from the inquiry, visibly upset, and took no further part.[8]

Unsurprisingly, the five hour cross-examination of Robert Rainbird produced more than a little vitriol and evasiveness. For example, when questioned by George Beattie, the solicitor acting on behalf of Beryl Mills, the following exchange occurred. Attempting to establish Rainbird's role in arranging the fatal trip, Mr Beattie asked why he (Rainbird) had said he knew nothing about the price to be charged for the boat and had not made arrangements concerning the charter, when Beryl Mills had already given evidence to the contrary.

'Mrs Mills has been through a very trying experience and it wouldn't be surprising if her memory wasn't coloured by her tragedy,' replied

6. *Falmouth Packet*, 6th January 1967.
7. *Falmouth Packet*, 16th December 1966.
8. Report of Court No. 8042 M.V. Darlwyne.

Rainbird.[9]

'Who do you suppose told Mrs Hicks to get all those sandwiches ready?' asked Mr Beattie.

'Mrs Mills often went into the kitchen to make hot drinks for her family and it would not be out of the ordinary for her to have mentioned sandwiches. Mrs Hicks had a free hand', came the response.[10]

Mr Beattie's questioning became more direct: 'I would suggest that what was happening in fact, was that you were arranging this trip for your guests ...'

'You can suggest what you like but that doesn't make it true', snapped Rainbird.[11]

When asked why his solicitor, Mr P H Langdon, had chosen not to cross-examine Beryl Mills on her evidence which contradicted his own, Robert Rainbird replied: 'My instructions were to spare Mrs Mills as much as possible, which apparently you are not prepared to do.'[12]

After the Christmas recess, the inquiry reconvened on Monday the 2nd of January 1967 and saw John Barratt take the witness stand. He gave evidence for four-and-a-half-hours and, according to news reports, was composed but spoke in a voice which at times became almost inaudible. He twisted his hands nervously as he stood in the witness box and often drew his right hand across his face. Once, Commissioner Naisby asked him if he wished to sit down but Barratt declined.[13]

At one stage, Mr Michael Thomas, the solicitor acting for the Board of Trade, asked him about the use of the *Darlwyne* for the 'rowdy' trip to view the Tall Ships Race.

'Did you at that time consider whether you were entitled to have such a trip in your boat?'

'I understood that as long as less than twelve passengers were carried it was quite in order', replied John Barratt.

---

9. *Falmouth Packet*, 23rd December 1966.
10. Ibid.
11. Ibid.
12. Ibid.
13. *Falmouth Packet*, 6th January 1967.

Mr Quentin Edwards, John Barratt's own solicitor, attempted to paint a more responsible picture and asked him: 'When you first knew that over 20 passengers were on board, were you dismayed?'

'Very much so', replied Barratt.[14]

But what was most crucial was to establish whether John Barratt actually owned the *Darlwyne* or had, as he had claimed, already sold her to Brian Bown. As Mr Thomas, for the Board of Trade put it to Barratt: 'It would have been so easy and the most natural thing in the world to have fended off the press and the Board of Trade by saying "it is nothing to do with me. I have sold the boat"'.

'I said nothing to anyone', replied Barratt.[15]

George Beattie, for Mrs Mills, then asked him how he would have reacted had the boat returned safe and sound, but Brian Bown had decided that he no longer wanted to buy her.

'I would have said that you made a deal. The deal was cut and dried. He was extremely pleased with the boat', suggested Beattie.[16]

Mr John Lawrence, acting for Mary Bown asked why, when he was so short of money, had Barratt not told Bown that he wanted part payment for the *Darlwyne* straight away. Barratt replied that he had tried for a better deal but Bown would go no further. Mr Lawrence said that it was surprising that with the considerable sums of money involved Barratt had not mentioned the alleged deal to a third party, such as Frank Lang or his daughter. Barratt replied that he had too much on his mind to discuss it with anyone. It was clear that with Brian Bown dead, John Barratt had no way of proving that he was not still the owner of the *Darlwyne*.[17]

As the inquiry drew to an end, Mr Beattie asked that the court find all three principal participants, John Barratt, Robert Rainbird and Brian Bown, responsible for the tragedy:

'Mr Barratt should have known what his boat was doing and the purpose for

14. Ibid.
15. Ibid.
16. Ibid.
17. Ibid.

> which it was being used. Skipper Bown had taken out the *Darlwyne* knowing full well he hadn't the right to do so, while the hotel proprietor, Mr Rainbird, was certainly responsible morally for not making sure that too many passengers were not put aboard the *Darlwyne* and giving instructions that she should keep in smooth water.'[18]

With a great deal of complex and contradictory evidence to consider, Mr Naisby and his advisors were further delayed because the Board of Trade was seeking legal advice on whether criminal proceedings should be brought against any or all of the main protagonists. Some headway was made when the Truro District Coroner, Mr Lawrence C Carlyon, was able to deliver a verdict on the deaths of all the *Darlwyne* victims, including the 19 who were never recovered, using a clause of the Coroners (Amendment) Act of 1926 which was specifically introduced for circumstances such as these. That verdict was death by misadventure. He stated that 'Good does come out of evil — now boating regulations will be more strictly observed.'[19]

On Monday the 13th of March 1967, Mr Naisby read the report of the Court of Inquiry findings to a hushed gathering of press and relatives at the old County Hall. Much of that report has already been discussed, but the most salient points of his conclusion, and that of his two assistants, are quoted from the proceedings here:

> '36. In considering any question of blame for this disaster the Court is not concerned with any breaches of Acts of Parliament or local regulations or the failure to perform any duties imposed by the Common Law except in so far as such breaches or failures are proved to have contributed to the disaster. The woefully inadequate supply of life saving appliances may not have contributed to the loss of life especially if, as seems probable, everyone on board the *Darlwyne* was in the wheelhouse and cabin and the vessel at the end suddenly foundered or capsized. The lack of distress signals may have done so if, in fact, there was

18. *Falmouth Packet*, 16th June 1967.
19. Ibid.

trouble with her engines or steering gear. That, however, is not sufficient to establish a causative wrongful act or default.

37. The Court is satisfied that the major cause of the disaster was the *Darlwyne* going on a voyage to sea when she was physically unfit to withstand the normal perils which she might expect to meet. The Court finds that the loss of the *Darlwyne* was contributed to by the wrongful act or default of the late Brian Michael Bown in negligently taking the *Darlwyne* to sea with passengers on board when the vessel was not fit to go to sea in open waters and by the wrongful act or default of her owner Mr John Campbell Maitland Barratt in failing to ensure that Mr Bown, his servant or agent, was specifically warned that the *Darlwyne* in her then state was not fit to go to sea in open waters.

38. The Court feels that the wrongful act or default on the part of Mr John Campbell Maitland Barratt calls for severe censure but that in all the circumstances of the case the maximum practicable amount which the Court can order Mr Barratt to contribute to the costs of this investigation is £500.

39. Having regard to the evidence in this case the Court is strongly of the opinion that all messages, whether verbal or by telephone, relating to any enquiry about a vessel received by the coastguards, should be recorded by them as required by paragraph 371 of the Instructions to Coastguards.

The Court is also of the opinion that further consideration should be given to the question as to whether anyone in charge of any kind of craft of a certain size should not be compelled to hold a licence enabling him or her to take charge of such craft and whether such licences should only be issued after an examination to test a person's fitness to be in control of such a craft.

Both the City of Truro and the Falmouth Harbour Commissioners have local regulations saying that persons in charge of a boat carrying passengers for hire must be licensed and that any craft carrying passengers for hire must also be licensed for that purpose and an examination is made of the craft concerned and permission given to carry so many passengers according to the size and

> condition of the craft. With the number of small craft proceeding within or out of or into these ports these are clearly provisions which it is difficult to enforce, and it is recommended that consideration should be given on a national basis to the need for there to be such regulations in all areas and how they are to be enforced.
>
> 40. The powers of local authorities to impose penalties for breach of their regulations which may affect the safety of life at sea date from the Victorian era and in the opinion of the Court are utterly inadequate in view of present-day conditions and values and it is suggested that consideration should be given to the question of enabling local authorities to increase these penalties drastically.'[20]

Brian Bown's widow, Mary, was deeply unhappy with the verdict. Speaking to the press outside the court she told the *Daily Mirror*: 'I am very disappointed. I am sure Brian would never have taken risks.'[21] She told the *Falmouth Packet*: 'My husband was a competent and experienced yachtsman quite capable, in my opinion, of skippering this trip.'[22]

John Barratt was devastated and considered appealing. 'I am not a rich man', he told the *Falmouth Packet* and he thought the findings 'rather unfair.'[23]

Robert Rainbird announced: 'I am vindicated.'[24]

---

20. Report of Court No. 8042 M.V. Darlwyne.
21. *Daily Mirror*, 14th March 1967.
22. *Falmouth Packet*, 17th March 1967.
23. Ibid.
24. Ibid.

‘The greatest griefs are those we cause ourselves.’

Sophocles

CHAPTER 7

Aftermath

The verdict of the inquiry hardly came as a shock, although the fact that Robert Rainbird was not found culpable is said to have surprised many and angered a few. Nevertheless, the law had spoken. But the press had not finished with Rainbird. On Friday the 21st of April 1967, the *Falmouth Packet* reported the breach of an enforcement order to cease using Greatwood as a hotel in May of 1963. It was only on the 25th of July 1966, six days before the *Darlwyne* tragedy, that the planning authority had gathered sufficient evidence to take legal action against Mr and Mrs Rainbird.[1]

As before, Robert Rainbird was represented by his solicitor, Mr P H Langdon from Torquay, who told the planning authority that Greatwood was a large old building which would become a white elephant if it could not be used as a hotel. Rainbird added that if it was not to be a hotel it would 'probably become a cow shed.' When asked to clarify this by Mr E R Austin, assistant solicitor to Cornwall County Council, he replied: 'If we don't use it as an hotel, it can be used as a pig farm or for any other purpose under the Agricultural Act.'

'You will do everything in your power to make Greatwood as obnoxious as possible?' asked Mr Austin.

1. *Falmouth Packet*, 21st April 1967.

'That is not what I said,' replied Rainbird, 'but pigs are becoming more remunerative and I may be going in for pigs if I cannot do this.'

The area planning officer, Mr R J K Relph, stepped in stating: 'The quite outstanding beauty of the Carrick Roads area is a national asset of the greatest importance, and it is considered that nothing must be permitted which in any way detracts from that beauty.'[2]

Mr Langdon agreed that it would be worse if Greatwood were to become derelict but added: 'But I do not think that would happen.'[3] He was wrong. What might be termed 'the *Darlwyne* effect' along with his inability to obtain the correct licences ultimately spelled the end for Greatwood as a hotel, and around 1970 Robert Rainbird abandoned it. It wasn't long before the fine old building was badly vandalised, both by squatters and by local people helping themselves to parts of it. The roof was completely stripped of its lead. One witness told me: 'There wasn't a floorboard left. You could see from the basement to the roof. There was hardly a boat in the Fal Estuary that didn't have a bit of Greatwood timber in it.'[4] Of course, Mr and Mrs Rainbird never actually owned Greatwood. The Gore-Langton family managed to sell it to a property developer who subsequently went bust and once more the squatters took over. Finally, it was sold again and developed into the luxury apartments that are still there today, although the Gore-Langton family received only a fraction of its value.

The repercussions of the *Darlwyne* disaster spread far beyond the leafy grounds of Greatwood House. The pleasure boat industry was badly hit, especially locally in Cornwall, where some lost entire days' charters and others went out of business altogether. It was estimated that bookings were down by 50%. The local boatmen certainly had a valid argument to make. In the press, the *Darlwyne* had frequently been referred to as a 'pleasure boat' but that was not the case. She was a privately owned, unlicensed motor cruiser. They wrote a strongly worded letter to the local papers, laying out the stringent safety conditions under which they operated.

2. Ibid.
3. Ibid.
4. Author interview with Chris Rendell, who lived in Mylor at the time of the incident.

'Sir — From recent letters it appears that the writers — and probably the public — are unaware of the 1965–66 regulations governing passenger boats and crews sailing from Falmouth piers and quays.

Briefly they are that: (1) The boats must be granted a licence by the borough council; (2) They must have passed the annual survey of the Board of Trade or the Harbour Commissioners; and (3) The skippers (either Board of Trade or 12 passenger boats) must have a current waterman's licence and the crew must also be licensed.

To apply for a waterman's licence a person must: (a) have previously been in charge of a passenger boat in Falmouth Harbour for not less than 12 months; (b) have been assistant to a waterman and engaged in the navigation of a passenger boat in Falmouth for not less than 12 months; (c) have experience in navigation of sea-going vessels and be able to handle and navigate a boat; and (d) must satisfy the Harbourmaster as to his capability and suitability to take charge of a passenger boat and have a general knowledge of the harbour and all regulations concerning Right of Way etc.

These regulations were brought in to improve the standards and I don't think that the public has any need to fear sailing from the recognized piers where there are pier masters to ensure that regulations are complied with.

I can also state that of the countless thousands of passengers I have seen sail from the Prince of Wales Pier since the war, every single one has been landed safely.

Stuart Nield, skipper, *Marina II*.'[5]

The regulations were certainly being enforced with renewed, or perhaps appropriate, zeal. For example, five shark fishing boats from Looe, about a third of the total fleet, had been banned by the Harbour Master, Mr J H Sarjeant, from putting to sea without first being fitted with the appropriate

5. *Falmouth Packet*, 23rd September 1966.

life rafts. The Board of Trade, whilst enforcing the regulations, at least tried to help implement them and asked commercial boat owners to contact them in order to speed up delivery of essential safety equipment.[6]

In Parliament, an amendment to the Criminal Justice Bill proposed to give some weight to the current regulations by increasing the paltry penalty of £5 for operating an unlicensed boat to a more punitive £50.[7] The pleasure boat industry in Cornwall was able to recover and soon enough it was thriving again, but the human cost of the tragedy was a constant presence in the lives of many people. The Reverend Frank Martin stayed in touch with many of the bereaved and is remembered with great fondness for his unwavering support.

Those relatives were keen to see a memorial of some description erected at Mylor to commemorate their loved ones. A team of craftsmen headed by local man John Phillips were commissioned to construct a memorial screen to be located in the church of St Mylor, by the small harbour. The relatives funded the project with a contribution from the Parish Council in recognition that local residents Joel and Amanda Hicks were among the dead.

The screen was officially dedicated on Sunday the 9th of April 1967. The church of St Mylor was packed as the friends and relations of the dead were joined by representatives of the Royal Navy, the RAF, the Police, the Board of Trade, several harbour masters, the Coastguard and the RNLI. The service was conducted by the Reverend Frank Martin, Dr Maurice Key, the Bishop of Truro, and Father D Collins representing the Catholic Church, of which the Tassell family were staunch members. At the end of the service, red tulips were placed beside the screen. They were the favourite flowers of Amanda Hicks.

The screen still stands today and is a beautiful thing. Carved from light oak with images of dolphins eternally frolicking in the waves across the top, there are usually flowers left beside it in memory of one or more of the victims. It is decorated with the following inscription:

---

6. *The Times*, 2nd August 1967.
7. *The Times*, 14th March 1967.

Lawrence Arthur Bent
Kathleen Bent
George Lawrence Bent
Brian Michael Bown
Roger Duncan Brock
Jean Brock
James Cowan
Dora Cowan
Susan Cowan
Mary Rose Dearden
George Edmonds
Amanda Jane Hicks
Joel Hicks
Arthur Raymond Mills
Jonathon David Mills
Janice Beverly Mills
Kenneth Arthur Robinson
Patricia Roome
Albert Russel
Margaret May Russel
John David Russel
Patricia Ann Russel
Jeffrey Claude Stock
Peter Lyon Tassell
Eileen Sybil De-Burgh Tassell
Susan Gail Tassell
Nicola Sarah Tassell
Frances Harriet Tassell
Lorraine Sandra Thomas
Malcolm Raymond Wright
Margaret Wright.

To the glory of God and in memory of thirty-one men women and children lost at sea in the motor vessel *Darlwyne* on 31st July 1966.

When the Bishop of Truro had read out the all names to the congregation, he finished with a biblical quote from the Song of Solomon, Chapter 8, Verse 7:

'Many waters cannot quench love; neither can floods drown it.'[8]

8. *Falmouth Packet*, 12th April 1967.

'And in the shadow-
less, unclouded glare
Deep blue above us fades
to whiteness where
A misty sea-line meets
the wash of air.'

John Betjeman, Cornish Cliffs

CHAPTER 8

The Land and the Sea
The Route the *Darlwyne* Took

Before the story moves on to the present day, it may be useful to recap the outward journey of the *Darlwyne* to try to tie in some of the many place names that have come up in the course of telling the story so far and may be confusing to those not well acquainted with Cornish geography.

The south coast of Cornwall is rightly famed for its breathtaking coastline, but its rivers can be every bit as beautiful. Those such as the Tamar, Fowey, Fal and Helford cut deep into the Cornish peninsula, often bounded by lush woodland and further upstream crossed by ancient stone bridges dating back many centuries. Mylor is a community in just such a location. It is a peninsula within a peninsula. To the north lies Restronguet Creek, to the south, Falmouth Harbour, and to the east, the Carrick Roads. Here, in the trees which line the estuary, sits Greatwood, from where the *Darlwyne* set off.

She headed south down the River Fal which, at over 30 metres, is one of the deepest natural harbours in the world. On her starboard side she will have passed the town of Falmouth, then, as now, a busy sea port catering for pleasure boats as well as large ships. Had the *Darlwyne* turned to starboard, she would have passed the Custom House Quay on her port side, where the first of the bodies was brought ashore. Continuing on this course, she would have arrived in Penryn where she was used as a houseboat and where Frank Lang worked on her. It was here that she was usually moored close to the house where John Barratt lived.

But she carried on south and entered Falmouth Bay where the raucous trip to view the Tall Ships Race took place. On her starboard side, the Lizard Peninsula stretches as far as the eye can see, its huge rampart interrupted only by the jagged rocks of the Manacles Reef, the site of over 50 wrecks. The Helford River cuts deep into the Lizard almost like a fjord. Frank Lang and Elizabeth Barratt took the *Darlwyne* there on her Whitsun sea trail.

On her port side she passed the mouth of the Percuil River and the picturesque village of St Mawes. This was where she was first taken when she was brought to Cornwall in 1962. Then she turned to port to round St Anthony's Head lighthouse with its squat, octagonal tower, and set a course to the northeast, being careful to avoid the complicated pinnacles and gullies of the Bizzies Reef, and crossing Gerrans Bay, towards Gull Rock, just off Nare Head. Gull Rock was frequently used as a reference point both for the Royal Navy search and for the investigation of the claim by Mrs Fuller, the eyewitness from Portloe, who believed that she had seen the *Darlwyne* heading towards it. Inshore, between Gull Rock and Nare Head lies the wreck of the German barque the *Hera* which sank in 1914. The *Darlwyne* could have safely passed over the top of this wreck which lies in 16 metres of water and is quite flat. But it is more likely that she stayed on the seaward side of Gull Rock by some margin to avoid the Whelps reef which runs from the base of the rock, off to the south.

Rounding Nare Head will have brought the *Darlwyne* into Veryan Bay, the prime focus of the search by HMS *Iveston* and the Royal Navy dive team. She would have altered course at this point to take a more easterly line in order to avoid Lath Rock, a large pinnacle which rises from the seabed at 25 metres to within a few metres of the surface and sits in the middle of the bay, passing Portloe as she did so. Once past Lath Rock, Porthluney Cove would have been visible on her port side with Caerhays Castle standing at the back of the beach. It was here that an eyewitness believed they had seen four people clinging to Diamond Rock, just to the east of the beach. The change of course to the east would be necessary too, to avoid the reefs around the looming promontory of Dodman Point.

At 114 metres tall, Dodman Point is the highest point of the south coast of Cornwall.[1] It is bounded to the west by Veryan Bay, and Mevagissey Bay to the east. The rock is dark grey, almost black in places, superficially resembling the hard serpentine granite found further west. But this is not igneous rock. The Dodman arose not from a volcano, coming instead from deep beneath an ancient sea as layers of mud and sand were compacted and heated by vast tectonic forces that thrust the seabed upwards, forming the Cornish peninsula.[2]

The headland is dominated by a huge Iron Age promontory fortress, at over 650 metres long one of the largest in Britain. In more modern times, a stone cross was erected on the summit in 1896 by the Reverend G Martin not as any sort of memorial, but as a navigational aid to seafarers. Nevertheless, every year, flowers are left there in memory of the dead of the *Darlwyne*, sometimes the red tulips beloved of Amanda Hicks, but more often any flowers in season. Offshore to the south of the Dodman lie two complicated reef systems known locally as the Field and the Bellows, which sit on top of a steep sided rock plateau. As the tide ebbs and flows over these reefs the sea is never still, even when there is not a breath of wind. When the wind begins to blow from almost any direction except the north, a nightmarish maelstrom of eddies and overfalls makes this small patch of sea a place to avoid for vessels of all sizes. So much so that this area has an old nickname that is still used by local fishermen to this day. Instead of the Dodman, they call it the Deadman.

The steep hike up to the cross on the summit affords a spectacular view of the south Cornish coast, but the real majesty of Dodman Point is revealed when it is seen from the sea. On the eastern flank, a jumble of boulders litters the grassy slope and reveals that a huge rockfall took place in the distant past, showing clear evidence of the friable nature of the compressed sandstone bedrock. But the western flank is altogether more imposing, a steep, solid buttress rises from sea level to the top of the

1. National Trust https://www.nationaltrust.org.uk/the-dodman
2. Author interview with Chris Rendell, who lived in Mylor and was a friend of Joel Hicks.

promontory and, when cloud and mist shrouds the summit, as it often does, it's easy to imagine this flanking an enormous alpine mountain.

The Dodman has long been associated with mariners returning home after a long voyage. The famous sea shanty 'Spanish Ladies', sung by Robert Shaw in the film *Jaws*, tells the tale of a British ship making her way back up the channel to her home anchorage in the Thames Estuary:

> 'So the first land we made, it is called the Deadman,
> Next Rame Head off Plymouth, Start, Portland and Wight,
> We sailed by Beachy, by Fairly and Dungeness,
> And then bore away for the South Foreland light.[3]'

Mariners are ambivalent about this place. Although it welcomed them home, it could also hold them in a deadly embrace, and the *Darlwyne* was by no means the first vessel to be lost in the vicinity. The jagged rocks and treacherous reefs were believed to be home to sirens who would whistle to beckon the unwary to their doom.

When giving evidence about sea conditions off Dodman Point to the Court of Enquiry, District Coastguard Officer William Adair pointed out the danger of the overfalls at the Field and Bellows reefs which most mariners were careful to avoid. Fishermen from Fowey described it a 'helluva place.'[4]

Whether the *Darlwyne* chose a route on the seaward or landward side of the Field and Bellows reefs is not known. What we do know is that with the weather already worsening, Brian Bown will have been able to see for himself that sailing over the top of them will have been highly ill-advised.

But the *Darlwyne* rounded the Dodman safely, keeping the fishing village of Gorran Haven at a safe distance on her port side to avoid the Gwineas (or Gwinges) Rocks which lie about a mile offshore. At this point she would have altered course again more to the north-northeast to cross Mevagissey Bay. We will never know for certain whether the *Darlwyne*

3. Traditional sea shanty.
4. Report of Court No. 8042 M.V. Darlwyne.

made a detour into Mevagissey, or even where this story originated. As I mentioned before, I have my doubts, but either way, early afternoon would have seen her keeping Gribben Head and St Austell Bay some distance from her port side in order to clear the last major obstacle on her journey, Cannis Rock. It was here that fisherman Ernest Holder had just caught a big fish when the *Darlwyne* passed by on its way out of the Fowey Estuary, which would now be clearly visible dead ahead with Fowey itself on the western side and Polruan opposite on the eastern side. It would then have been a straightforward task to disembark the passengers at either Town Quay or the adjacent Albert Quay had the faulty steering allowed. This much we know. For the next 50 years, where the *Darlwyne* went next would be a complete mystery.

A picket boat, the *Green Parrot*, identical in design to the *Darlwyne*.

Courtesy of the British Military Powerboat Team.

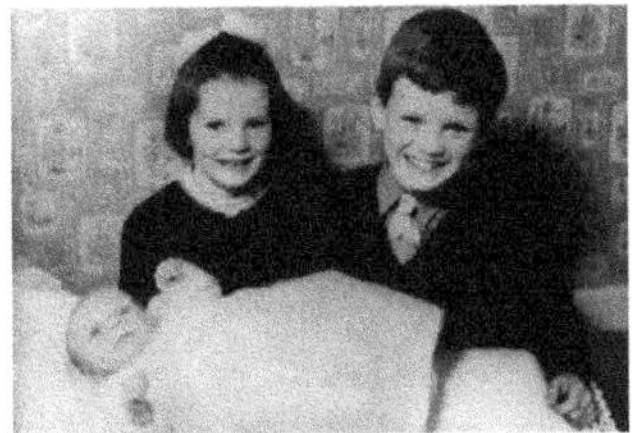

Robert Rainbird. Raymond and Beryl Mills on their wedding day, courtesy of the *Southport Visiter*. David and Janice Mills with baby Lisa.

Greatwood Quay.

Courtesy of Mark Milburn.

The search being coordinated at St Just Airport.

The recovered tender.

Coffins being unloaded at Falmouth.

Helicopter winchman.

Nick Lyon and Mark Milburn.

Courtesy of Jeremy Hibbard.

Nick briefing divers Felicity Flashman and Katrina Mace.

Courtesy of Mark Milburn.

Dodman Point.

Courtesy of Julie Lyon.

Divers Mark Milburn and Dave Gibbins making final checks, while Jeff Goodman films on a GoPro camera.

Courtesy of Jeremy Hibbard.

Nick with a possible granite sett.

Courtesy of Felicity Flashman.

Anchor.

Courtesy of Mark Milburn.

Metalwork.

Courtesy of Mark Milburn.

The memorial in Mylor church.

'The way to find a needle in
a haystack is to sit down.'

Beryl Markham

CHAPTER 9

Searching the Past

I have never met anyone quite like Mark Milburn before and neither, I suspect, has anyone else. I had first encountered him on a scuba diving internet forum and was always impressed by his wide-ranging knowledge. When Julie and I moved to Cornwall in 2009, we actually met in person. He was immensely helpful, particularly as we had decided, unwisely, to move our furniture and belongings ourselves. Mark immediately offered the loan of a van he had bought on eBay for £300. During the three trips from Devon, the head gasket failed, one tyre punctured, a wheel came off and, to cap it all, I put the wrong fuel in and was charged £175 to have it pumped out. Of course, none of those things were Mark's fault, but I was left with an indelible impression that Mark was generous if somewhat eccentric. As he says himself, the filter which most of us have to prevent random thoughts from leaving our brains via our mouths is missing in his case. This means that the most straightforward exchanges of information can be extremely prolonged. But if you have enough time, you can tap in to a veritable encyclopaedia of knowledge, particularly regarding diving and shipwrecks.

Mark runs a dive centre in Mabe, just outside Falmouth, called Atlantic Scuba. Situated in a disused quarry filled with shipping containers which are rented out for storage, the dive centre occupies two of three business units. There is a small dive shop and dive school from which various instructors, aside from Mark, work part-time. A tiny workshop houses servicing and testing equipment for cylinders and regulators and there are two compressors to fill diving cylinders with air or other gasses. All areas of the shop, store, classroom, and workshop are stuffed full of old dive gear, books, and artefacts recovered from the seabed. Even outside the shop there is assorted wreckage, from a pile of cannon balls to the hatch from a U-boat. A short drive away at Mylor, from where the *Darlwyne* set off, Mark keeps his charter boat, an eight-metre-long rigid inflatable boat (RIB) called *Stingray.*

There is a saying that the way to make a million in the dive industry is to start with five million. Some people do make a decent living but that was never really the goal for Mark. He has a dive business because he simply loves to go diving. But what sets his business apart from others in the area is his limitless enthusiasm for variety. He is always on the lookout for new sites, new activities and especially for new wrecks. That has always suited me perfectly, which is why we began to collaborate. Some people used to think that I worked for Mark, but the truth is no money ever changed hands. I used to help him with the running of his business and, in the process, I never ran out of things to write about. This odd symbiosis lasted for a number of years, until I relocated to Orkney.

But if there's one area of the diving industry circus that Mark has a particular passion for, it's the media, especially film and television. When he found a camera on the bed of the Helford River and managed to extract the memory card, he appealed on local news for anyone recognising the people in the pictures to come forward. Unexpectedly, the story went global. Mark's daughter Natasha was doing voluntary work in an orphanage in Peru and was astonished to see him featured on the news there. Then, whilst scallop diving nearby in the Helford estuary, he found what turned out to be a German Second World War parachute mine, the largest unexploded bomb ever discovered in Cornwall. When the Royal Navy bomb disposal team arrived to blow it up, that too was a major story and Mark was well and truly bitten by the media bug. Since then, we have worked on various TV projects for programmes such as *Countryfile* and *The One Show*, when we were filmed removing a discarded fishing net from the Manacles reef.[1] He began to wear the insulting epithet 'media whore' like a badge of honour! But it became clear that apart from getting our ugly mugs on the television, there was a more tangible benefit to involving ourselves in these projects. That is that if we had something to do that was suitably interesting to the viewing public, the television companies, particularly the BBC, could help us meet the expenses incurred.

It was around this time that fate intervened in the shape of a chance conversation on the quayside at Mylor … One morning in late spring, 2016, I rolled up at Atlantic Scuba to help out with some cylinder testing to find Mark sat behind his desk, gazing at the computer screen.

'Morning', he said. 'Ever heard of the *Darlwyne*?'

'Darwin? As in Charles Darwin?' I replied.

'No, *D-a-r-l-w-y-n-e*. It's a wreck. Sank in 1966 with dozens of people killed.'

I was taken aback at this because it had sunk within my lifetime and I had never heard of it. Mark told me that he had been chatting with an instructor from Mylor sailing school who had asked him if he had ever tried looking for the *Darlwyne*. He asked the seemingly random question because a television producer called Jeremy Hibbard had used one of the sailing school's boats to film a documentary about the events of 1966, presented by veteran broadcaster, Angela Rippon. He found himself wondering if any divers had searched for the *Darlwyne*. Like me, Mark was astounded that he had never heard of it, but in typical fashion he hit the internet running and so was able to give me an outline sketch of the story.

The first thing we established was that, as neither of us are interested in football, we had to check the date of the 1966 World Cup Final! Then we turned to the *Darlwyne* itself and it became obvious that this was a very small wreck but that was about it. Neither of us could imagine how so many people could be carried by such a small boat. We weren't even sure what a picket boat was, and I began to make a list of things to read up on. It was a list which grew rapidly. With every question answered, it seemed another five would rear up. It soon became clear that for such a

1. *The One Show*, BBC, 2nd November 2015.

recent and tragic story, information was amazingly sparse, in fact there seemed to be only one book on the subject, namely *The Mysterious Loss of the Darlwyne: A Cornish Holiday Tragedy* by Martin Banks[2] and a chapter in *The Cruel Cornish Sea* by the late David Mudd.[3] I had copies on order that day and Mark had already contacted Jeremy to arrange a meeting the following week to discuss whether a search for the wreck and a documentary for the series *Inside Out* was feasible.

The first meeting took place on Thursday the 8th of June at Atlantic Scuba. Jeremy arrived right on time and his enthusiasm was impressive and infectious. As well as Neil Tugwell, the surface camera man, he had brought Martin Banks, the author of *The Mysterious Loss of the Darlwyne* with him. Martin is rightly regarded as an expert on all things *Darlwyne*-related, so his input was invaluable and he gave freely of his time and knowledge. This first filming session consisted of various theories and scenarios being discussed between Mark, Martin and me. There was a certain amount of artifice in evidence, as there always is with filming, but as Martin is a professional actor he was much more at home with saying the same thing over several takes than Mark and I. It has to be said, too, that this was unscripted, and we were very much making things up as we went along. Nevertheless, the session threw up some fascinating possibilities, and more importantly, some consensus about the location to be investigated.

The very nature of the seabed off Dodman Point meant that there were no sufficiently accurate paper nautical charts available. The area between the Field and Bellows reefs and the Dodman itself is a complex maze of gullies and pinnacles which would have been all but impossible to survey safely from all but the smallest vessel. This also meant that at the time of the sinking, due to their size, the naval ships engaged in the search would not have been able to search this patch of seabed in a methodical way. Fortunately, technology came to the rescue. In recent years a number of systems have been developed whereby hydrographic data from any vessel

2. Tamar Books, 2014.
3. Bossiney Books, 1981.

fitted with a particular navigation equipment can be collated in the cloud and made available to any other vessel or user subscribing to the system. This means that huge amounts of data can be shared, making information about depths and seabed features incredibly detailed and accurate. We were using just such a system known as Navionics and it proved invaluable.

Given what we already knew about the sea conditions at the time, and the poor state and gross overloading of the *Darlwyne*, we theorised that she was not likely to have made any headway into Veryan Bay. Again, this was all on the balance of probability; there was no certainty. Then we turned to the grim but important matter of the distribution of the bodies. The calculations we made were hardly scientific, but a number of reasonable suppositions and a few sparse facts were factored into our theory.

The first question to ask was: Why were all the bodies discovered to the east of Dodman Point? Did this mean that the wreck must also be to the east, in Mevagissey Bay for example? Given the earlier of the eyewitness accounts and the relative calm in Mevagissey Bay at the time, it seemed unlikely, but no possibility could be completely excluded at this stage. In order to answer that question, we had to get to grips with the complex tidal streams around the Dodman. Often, the tidal information given for certain positions indicated by tidal diamonds on the paper charts can vary considerably only a very short position from each particular diamond, particularly where reefs and rock pinnacles interrupt the tidal stream. With this in mind, we concentrated on the incoming or flood tide because this must have been the tide which carried the bodies, given their eventual location; but why was this? Why didn't the ebb tide also distribute them in the other direction?

This question was a real problem for us until we considered the case of Jean Brock, the fifth victim to be found. Despite having 'deep drowned' she was wearing a lifebelt, and although it was one slightly below the Board of Trade regulation size she was still buoyant. This suggested that the victims were contained within the wreck and only washed out during the flood tide. Again, we wondered why that should be. It may have been a function of the way the wreck was lying but there was another possibility. It may have been that the wreck itself was sheltered from the ebb tide by a rock or reef and therefore only subject to the influence of the flood tide. By extrapolating the information from various tidal diamonds, as well as picking the brains of people with better local knowledge than ourselves, we calculated that the flood tide to the south of the Dodman changed direction by 44 degrees throughout its duration. It was within this arc that all the bodies were discovered. Now we had to work out its point of origin and tie it in with a reef behind which there was shelter from the ebb tide. We were still looking for a needle in a haystack, but the haystack had shrunk considerably from its former size of 15 square miles.

We then came to discuss the matter of the alleged eyewitness accounts. Whilst never discounting them completely, it was easy to pick holes. It may well be that the farmer, Leslie Smith, *did* see the *Darlwyne* from his field on the west side of Dodman Point and the two men fishing off Gorran Haven may also have done so. But we know that she will have passed that position in any case. Where she went next is the real question.

The report by Mrs Fuller, who claimed to have seen the *Darlwyne* from Portloe, immediately raises suspicion because she reported seeing a blue boat whereas the *Darlwyne*'s hull was white. Then there was the question of the visibility. We found it quite unlikely that in weather conditions as poor as those of the 31st of July anyone could have confidently identified the *Darlwyne* at any distance. Nevertheless, we plotted the most easterly lines of sight from Portloe and Hemmick respectively, and concluded that whether or not the reports were accurate or even true, the lines of sight converged very close to where we intended to search. We made a note to check the feasibility of these sightings when we were out in the boat.

Then we turned our attention to the report of the four people clinging to Diamond Rock. Whilst this was taken seriously at the time, it subsequently played no part in the court of enquiry. We reasoned that, on balance, it was highly unlikely that this incident was connected with the *Darlwyne*. Quite apart from the distance that four people would have to swim from Dodman Point to Porthluney Cove, there was no reason why anyone would be clinging to a rock just offshore when a flat, sandy beach was only metres away. Were these people local swimmers? Were they actually seals? Were they there at all? We shall never know for sure, but we were reasonably confident that these were not likely to be victims of the *Darlwyne* tragedy.

Discussion of the victims threw up a subject that we had all been avoiding, namely the question of what we would do if we discovered human remains. We consulted our archaeological advisor, Dr David Gibbins, and he wisely suggested we look but not touch. With all the victims of the *Darlwyne*, including the 19 who were never recovered, having been declared dead by the coroner at the time, the legal issues were less complex than they might have been. However, morally we felt strongly that it was better to record the presence of remains and leave them undisturbed than it was to recover them in the hope of making an identification of any individual.

By now it was clear to me that this was a wreck story like no other I had ever dealt with. Jeremy and Martin had already been bitten by the *Darlwyne* bug, of course, but I, too, found myself lying awake at night, trying to piece together the many confusing parts of the puzzle. The decision to find out as much as I could, whether or not this information was useful in locating the wreck, was not a difficult one to make. I had found Martin's book difficult to put down and I hoped that we could add a little more to this fascinating story. But that meant doing some serious research, something that doesn't come easily to me. Fortunately, my wife Julie is an old hand at it and we began to haunt various libraries and archives.

Initially, we spent a great deal of time in the National Maritime Museum in Falmouth. Astonishingly, as luck would have it, there was a temporary exhibition telling the story of the *Darlwyne* in one of the smaller galleries. This proved particularly useful as I was able to make a note of which editions of the contemporary newspapers to track down. There was also an area of the gallery in which the Movietone newsreel about the disaster was being shown. I watched it until I could repeat the commentary verbatim, each time finding the scenes of the coffins being brought ashore and the deserted Greatwood House particularly moving (*see page 61*).

In the rear of the museum sits the Bartlett Library. The core of that collection is some 19,000 books accumulated since 1945 by Mr J V Bartlett and bequeathed to the museum. As well as books on all aspects of seafaring, it holds an extensive archive of magazines and periodicals, as well as various directories, including *Lloyds Register* dating from 1788 to the present and the *Mercantile Shipping Register* from 1860 onwards. It was in the latter that Julie found the details for the *Darlwyne* which had eluded me for weeks.

We also spent a significant amount of time in the Cornwall Studies Centre in Redruth. This proved to be an invaluable resource as it holds the entire archive of the *Falmouth Packet* newspaper, as well as the transcript of the Court of Inquiry into the loss of the *Darlwyne*. Included in this were some photographs which I had never seen before, and it was a fascinating and somewhat eerie experience to put faces to some of the names about whom I had read so much. I found myself, as I had at the Maritime Museum, staring intently into the inscrutable face of Robert Rainbird and wondering just what he was thinking.

It is often said that the best place to find a shipwreck is in a library, but that was not so in the case of the *Darlwyne*. It struck us both as ironic that it was actually more difficult to trace the details of a modern wreck than one a century old, even though the loss of life had been terrible. So, for the purposes both of necessity and filming the documentary, the time had come to take the search out of the archives and into the sea.

‘I must go down to the sea again,
for the call of the running tide,
Is a wild call and a clear call
that may not be denied.’

John Masefield, Sea Fever

CHAPTER 10

Shrinking the Haystack

The task of finding a shipwreck anywhere is not an easy one, but finding a shipwreck in British waters carries additional challenges. Firstly, there is the weather. Whilst the influence of the waves decreases with depth, actually being out at sea in a boat in rough seas is at best unpleasant and at worst dangerous.

Once in the water, waves can render a surfacing diver invisible to the boat crew. Of course, the same thing applies to fog, only more so. Wave action can also stir up the seabed substrate, reducing visibility dramatically. After the ferocious storms of the winter of 2012–13, the underwater visibility took two years to return to normal. Rain can also affect visibility as it swells rivers and washes their burden of silt out to sea.

Then there are the tides. The strength and direction of the tidal streams in Britain vary greatly according to location, date, and the nuances of the tidal cycle. A tidal stream flowing faster than one knot (one nautical mile per hour) is all but impossible to swim against for any length of time. Tidal streams around the British Isles can often exceed five knots. It is possible to dive in such conditions, but the diver is compelled to be carried by the current. This is called a drift dive. It can actually be a useful way of covering a lot of ground with minimal effort, but the diver has no choice about the direction of travel and stopping to examine a find may not always be possible. Of course, we were aware of all this before we embarked on our search and wondered if there was any way in which we could further reduce our search area to offset the existing difficulties. As luck, or possibly fate, would have it, there was.

Julie and I had carried out a significant amount of research by this stage, but it seemed that every answer produced another set of questions. As a full-time college lecturer, there were other demands on her time and I simply didn't know where to look. I often read passages from Martin Banks' book and wondered how on Earth he'd found that particular witness or piece of information. It took me a frankly embarrassing length of time to realise that I had a very valuable resource right under my nose who might be able to help.

It's a curious feature of the social media age that people can have friends whom they've never actually met. Julie Skentelbery was one of mine. She's a presenter on BBC Radio Cornwall and had previously worked on local television, coincidentally with Jeremy Hibbard. She lives on a beautiful yacht moored in Falmouth with her husband Andy, who is a boat builder. We had a couple of mutual friends on Facebook and soon discovered that we had a similarly anarchic sense of humour. I mentioned the *Darlwyne* project and documentary to her, and was practically ordered to turn up at the BBC studios at Phoenix Wharf in Truro that week to be interviewed!

Of course, I could see the advantage in this, as an appeal for personal memories or other information could prove helpful for the search, but I had little idea just how beneficial that would turn out to be. The fact that the interview was on Friday the 13th of May didn't exactly help to steady my nerves, but Julie was the quintessential presenter and immediately put me at my ease as she teased the story of the disaster and the search from me. I live ten minutes' drive from the studio, but by the time I arrived home there were already several emails for me.

The first that I answered was from the lady who, as a teenager, had been on holiday with her three friends and who had missed the trip because they left their radio at the bus stop. The next was from Dene Berryman, who had been asked by Robert Rainbird to participate in the fatal voyage with her brother, and whose mother wouldn't let her go. I subsequently interviewed her at her home in Penzance. This was proving astonishingly valuable, but more was to come. I received a message from a man called Mark who asked me to telephone him that evening, which I did. I asked him what information he had and he simply said, 'I know where the *Darlwyne* is.' I tried not to sound sceptical. I had already come across plenty of people who had made this claim. I asked him how he knew this. He told me that his father had worked on a scallop dredger operating out of Fowey some 30 years previously. Whilst they were working close to Dodman Point, they had dredged up part of a wooden boat. I asked him what made him suspect that this wreckage was from the *Darlwyne*. In a matter-of-fact tone he said, 'because it was the entire transom and it had 'Darlwyne' written on it.'

I was literally dumbstruck, completely unable to know what to say for a second or two. Having partially regained my composure, I asked him if his father had kept the wreckage or photographed it. 'Nah,' he said, 'those Fowey fishermen are a superstitious lot and couldn't get it over the side fast enough.' I had gone from elated to crestfallen in seconds but asked him if he knew where the transom had been dredged up. 'I can't be exact', he told me, 'but roughly a third of a mile south by southwest of the Dodman.' I thanked him profusely and as soon as I had put the phone down I reached for the Admiralty chart of the area. The point that Mark had described was exactly in the centre of our intended search area.

There then followed a frustrating delay while the wind persistently blew in every direction but the one we needed, namely from the north. Eventually the prevailing south-westerly backed round to the northwest and eased enough to make the first dive sortie viable. On Thursday the 16th of June 2016, conditions were ideal, and the dive team and film crew assembled at Mylor marina. It has to be said that even at this stage, we were not at all confident about actually finding the wreck of the *Darlwyne* and the focus of the documentary was very much on telling the story leading up to her loss. Having said that, what we lacked in overt optimism we made up for in determination.

Whilst my research was inevitably concerned with the historical narrative, there were some potentially useful practical aspects to it. For example, knowing that the hull was of double diagonal construction might help identify any timbers we may have found. I also sought out pictures of the Perkins engines and the two anchors and shared them around the group. It was obvious to all of us that finding any of the ballast would be particularly useful. Pig iron would be difficult to spot after 50 years on the seabed, but it was still worth keeping an eye out for. It seemed to me that the granite setts might be a more likely sighting. Knowing that the rock which formed Dodman Point was compressed sandstone, it may be that a piece of granite, especially one which had been worked by hand, might be relatively easy to spot. To that end, on one of my previous visits to the Falmouth Maritime Museum, I had photographed some granite setts which were on display, and laminated the picture to take with us on the boat.

Having used the Navionics software to produce a highly detailed chart of our target area, we prepared to set sail, once Jeremy and Neil had filmed brief interviews with Mark and me.

To paraphrase the famous line from *Jaws* we were clearly going to need a bigger boat. Roomy though *Stingray* is, with five search divers, two surface film crew, one underwater cameraman, his safety diver and dive supervisor, and all the associated equipment, it was somewhat snug to say the least. That equipment included sufficient cylinders for two dives each, the surface camera gear, four underwater camera systems, diver-to-surface communication systems for the cameraman and safety diver, and plenty of food and drink!

The five divers were Mark, myself, Colin Stratton, Katrina Mace and Felicity Flashman. Jeff Goodman was the underwater cameraman and the safety diver and dive supervisor (who were present because Jeff was technically at work and therefore bound by the rules of the Health and Safety Executive) were Alex and Rob, hired by Jeremy from the prestigious Waterproof Media film company.[1]

The sea was calm as we left Mylor, with only a few ripples from the light wind. Just moments after leaving the marina, Greatwood House became visible through the trees on our port side and it made a truly evocative

1 www.divesolutions.co.uk

sight. This was the same view that passengers on board the *Darlwyne* will have seen astern as, like ourselves, they turned south and headed down the Carrick Roads towards the open sea. To be following exactly the same course as the *Darlwyne*, on the way to search for her, was an experience like no other wreck hunt I have participated in.

Mark guided *Stingray* round St Anthony's Head and once past Zone Point we were able to judge the conditions we would be facing. We had been caught out at this point before. With just a little less north and a little less east in the wind than had been forecast, our plans may have to have been put on hold. As it was, conditions were practically perfect, and the twin outboard engines roared into life as we crossed Gerrans Bay at 20 knots. We rarely venture any further than Gull Rock — to dive the wreck of the *Hera* — due to the amount of fuel it takes, but we passed it to port as we sped on into Veryan Bay.

Here was an opportunity to examine some of the eyewitness accounts more closely. At a point about one third of the distance between Gull Rock and Dodman Point, we were roughly in the position where Mrs Fuller said that she saw the *Darlwyne* on the evening of the sinking, yet the village of Portloe where she lived, was barely visible and we were in near perfect conditions. It seemed quite implausible that anyone could have identified a particular vessel at that range in pouring rain with blowing spray.

Before long we were drawing close to the towering promontory of Dodman Point. Using the various electronic position fixing systems on board *Stingray*, Mark manoeuvred the boat into the spot which his namesake had described as being the location at which the transom had been dredged up. When we were a third of a mile south by southwest of the Dodman, we gazed intently at the echo sounder and side scan sonar. We were crestfallen to discover that we were over a jagged seabed of rocks, pinnacles and gullies. This was not scallop fishing ground, so this can't have been where the transom was discovered.

But we soon reasoned that of the two measurements, the bearing was likely to be more precise than the estimate of distance, which is notoriously difficult to do accurately at sea. We therefore decided to head further out on that bearing and, at just over half a mile from the Dodman, the sounder revealed that we were on flat sand—prime scallop fishing ground. This correlated well with the position which we had earmarked as our search area and, therefore, this was where we would dive.

Just as on the day that the *Darlwyne* sank, we were in a period of gentle neap tides, but at the Dodman the sea is seldom still; in fact, accurate tidal prediction is all but impossible here. We determined that we were over a wide, flat-bottomed, sandy gully, some 800 metres long by 300 metres wide and an even 27 metres deep, running roughly northeast. We chose to begin our search on the northern edge of the gully and dropped a shotline to mark the centre of the search area. We watched the buoy on the line carefully. It indicated that the tide was running a little, but diving would be possible.

Mark and Colin would be first to submerge whilst I drove the boat. This actually meant that four divers would be in the water in the first wave, as Jeff would be filming them, and he would have to be accompanied by a safety diver as he was technically at work.

Neil filmed as the four divers kitted up. This took longer than it normally would as the surface-to-diver communication systems had to be fitted and tested. The divers rolled off the boat, swam to the nearby shotline (divers hate swimming on the surface, as it expends unnecessary energy, so I had manoeuvred the boat as close to the buoy as I could). After exchanging signals, they sank out of sight.

The mood on the boat was one of eager anticipation mixed with frustration at not being in the water ourselves. With the sea calm enough to see the divers' bubbles coming to the surface, all I could do was gently steer the boat around them, so that I would be reasonably close when they came back up. When the divers surfaced, they reported that visibility was reasonably good, but they had found no evidence of a wreck.

The first team sat out their surface interval to allow some of the nitrogen dissolved in their tissues to dissipate. I briefed Felicity and Kat on what we should be looking for and showed them the picture of the granite sett from the Maritime Museum. Felicity prepared her camera before we all donned our diving equipment and when we were ready, Mark motored over to the shotline and we rolled over the side of the boat.

The visibility was as Mark had said, and the shotline could be seen for some seven or eight metres below us as we descended into the light green water. We arrived at the seabed at 27 metres and saw that the shot weight was resting on coarse, light coloured sand. I set a compass course to the northwest in order to take us to the northern edge of the gully. The sand was barren and featureless for some time, until we came across a series of deep furrows running perpendicular to our course and disappearing into the gloom in both directions. These were clearly the tracks left by scallop dredging. This is not normally cause for celebration amongst divers as this method of fishing is indiscriminate and can cause serious habitat damage, but in this case it was further evidence that we may be in the right place.

Continuing on our way, we soon encountered the beginnings of the reef which marked the northern edge of the gully. We elected to turn to the right, keeping the reef on our left, and swam in a line to search the reef edge. The reef itself is a beautiful example of its type, liberally populated with soft corals and teeming with pollock and various species of wrasse. Looking upwards, a shoal of horse mackerel was hunting in midwater. But this was no scenic dive, we had a job to do. Kat spotted a length of electric cable. With any man-made object being a potential piece of evidence here, I examined it carefully. It bore no marine growth and at any rate would not be of much use in isolation, so we left it.

Just as we resumed swimming, we noticed that the current seemed to have picked up and we drifted with it along the reef edge. Then something caught my eye. It was a shape that just seemed out of place. I turned inelegantly against the current, kicking up a cloud of sand and destroying the view of the object. I settled on the seabed and waited for the tide to wash the sand cloud away. When it did so, the seabed was bare. I swam forward a couple of metres and found my mystery object. There was no doubt that it looked out of place here. With the rest of the reef edge solid and jagged, this was a small rock of a different colour to the reef and it was square with straight edges and a flat top. Was this one of the granite setts used to ballast the *Darlwyne*? It was slightly bigger than the ones in the Maritime Museum, but tantalising nonetheless. I sent up my delayed surface marker buoy as a signal to the boat, and we ascended to six metres to carry out our decompression stop.

Back on the boat, I discussed the rock with Jeremy and Mark. It looked incongruous but was it just an unusually shaped natural feature? At any rate, it seemed reasonable to stick to this area for the second dive. Mark and Colin dropped in just where I had sent up the buoy. By now, the tidal stream would not allow any choice as to the direction in which the divers would swim, but as luck would have it it was the direction we wanted. They drifted along the strip of sand between the reef edge and the dredge tracks, but after 30 minutes they had found nothing and ascended back to the boat.

For our second dive, Felicity, Kat and I decided to drop in a little upstream of where we estimated the stone block to be in an attempt to relocate it. As soon as we began to descend, it became clear that the strength of the tide would only allow a passing glimpse, even if we landed right on the top of it. Unfortunately for us, there had been subtle shift in the direction of the tide with the result that we were gradually carried away from the edge of the reef and back towards the scallop dredge tracks. Realising this, we decided to return to the surface.

As we started back to Mylor harbour, we discussed the day's diving. Firstly, the dredge marks were an encouraging sign that we were very likely to be in the right area. This was the only area of seabed close to our target area where scallop dredging could have been carried out and the transom had been raised by a scallop dredger. But then there was the issue of the rock. Could it have been a granite sett? I was not prepared to commit myself one way or the other, but it certainly seemed out of place.

We were in an awkward situation. We had wanted to do our best to find some evidence of the *Darlwyne* before the 31st of July: the 50th anniversary of her loss. Jeremy had liaised with some of the relatives of the deceased and organised a memorial ceremony to take place at sea. Was our gully where the ceremony should take place? It seemed to us that it was the likely site of the sinking, but knowing where a vessel sank is not the same as finding the wreck. In fact, it comes as a surprise to many people that some wrecks end up miles from where they actually went down. Take the case of *UB-81*. This was a 650-ton German U-boat on her maiden voyage in 1917. She struck a mine off the Isle of Wight and sank. Between the date of her sinking and 1989, the wreck was actually moved over 15 miles by the tide. A 12½-ton wooden wreck that had been trawled over could therefore have been moved a considerable distance. But we still had the evidence of the transom and the distribution of the bodies by the tide as the only real indicators of where we needed to be looking. We unanimously agreed that we would need to come back and have another look.

‘If I have ever made any valuable discoveries, it has been owing more to patient attention, than to any other talent.’

Isaac Newton

CHAPTER 11

The Wreck

If the voyage from Mylor to Dodman Point had been an evocative re-tracing of the *Darlwyne*'s fatal journey, then there were parallels, too, between our search and that of the Royal Navy. Like them, we were soon hampered by bad weather. It doesn't have to be blowing a hurricane to make conditions unsuitable off the Dodman. Such is the treacherous topography of land and seabed that, as soon as conditions begin to deteriorate even moderately, it is no place for boats or divers to be. So, following the first day's diving, we were continually postponing the subsequent dive as the weather repeatedly let us down.

Of course, there were other factors, too, such as the availability of personnel, as most of the participants had work or study commitments to meet. But the wait was extremely frustrating, especially with the deadline of the 50th anniversary and the memorial ceremony looming ever closer. As always, Jeremy was apparently calm and organised, but with his documentary lacking a definite ending he must have been worried. I had even considered borrowing another boat in case there was a weather window on a day when Mark was busy.

With time running short, the weather did indeed give us the break we needed and, at short notice, we made our second search on the 22nd of July. Coincidentally, this was my 4,000th dive, so I was particularly hopeful that we might have cause to celebrate. With Jeff unable to join us, we would have to do our own filming, but what we would lose in video expertise, we would gain in boat space, as there was no requirement for the additional safety diver and dive supervisor. Kat was also unavailable, but her place was taken by Izabela Konkel, whose keen eye for scallops could be retrained to look for wreckage.

It was not just time that was against us, the tide was also proving difficult and the slack water window would only allow one dive per team. There was a little more chop than on the previous dives, but the conditions were still quite acceptable. We arrived on site about 20 minutes before calculated slack water (which is usually the ideal time to dive). This time, we elected to search the opposite side of the gully, close to the steep plateau on which the Field and Bellows reefs sit. The shotline has two buoys attached to indicate tidal flow and, when it was deployed the smaller buoy instantly disappeared below the surface, which meant that the tide was still running hard. However, after 20 minutes had passed it had still not reappeared. Clearly, the Dodman was living up to its reputation for being unpredictable.

Now we had a dilemma. Should we wait and see if the ferocious tide eased off, or alter our plan and drift dive along the gully? We chose to wait another 15 minutes and our decision was proven correct, as both buoys were then on the surface, indicating that the tide had eased, though not slackened off altogether. Mark and Colin dived first again. I dropped them just upstream of the shotline so that the current would carry them to the buoy and watched as they disappeared down the line.

I tried to keep the boat close to the surfacing bubbles, driving at minimum power to conserve fuel and give the divers some respite from the roar of the engines. As often happens in areas of jagged and complex reefs, it soon became clear that although the tide had slackened off at the surface, it hadn't run out of steam at depth. Both sets of bubbles had begun to move faster and further apart. In a normal, recreational diving situation, separation is dealt with by both divers surfacing in order to reunite and dive again or abandon the dive, depending on the depth and time they have completed at that point. But we had planned for this eventuality, and had an understanding that any of the divers trained in solo diving techniques and equipped with extra air supplies — such as Mark, Colin and myself — could dive solo if the conditions required it.

After half-an-hour, both divers deployed their surface marker buoys, which demonstrated to us just how far they had drifted and how far apart they now were. I picked up Colin first, who reported that he had seen no evidence of a wreck. The disappointment on the boat was palpable. I turned it around and motored over to Mark. As always, his video camera was the first thing to be handed in to the boat. When Mark pulled himself up over the side and sat down, he took his mask off to reveal a strange, almost disbelieving expression. He said quite simply 'I may have found it'.

There was an excited scramble to crowd around the video screen to see what he had filmed. In bright daylight it was too difficult to make much sense of the images, so Mark told us that there was an anchor of the correct size for the *Darlwyne* with some chain attached, an anchor winch, some metal pipe and some wood, heavily damaged by ship worm. There was now no doubt about where my team would be diving!

Mark dropped us upstream of the position in which he estimated the wreckage to be, so we could drift over it when we reached the bottom. As we rolled in over the side of the boat, Felicity bobbed up looking very worried. It seemed that the leak indicator on her camera housing had been triggered and she rushed over to the boat with several thousand pounds worth of now vulnerable camera gear held above her head. This was a blow as her role had been to photograph any finds, but Izabela also had a small GoPro camera and that would have to do.

Once we were reunited at the shotline, we exchanged OK signals and sank down the line. We were a little further from the reef than I had anticipated, so with no obvious datum point, I decided that we should conduct a circular search. Using this method, the diver secures a line from a reel to a fixed object, in this case the shotline weight, and swims in a circle around the object. After one sweep is complete, the line is extended a little each time to increase the search area. Being flanked by Felicity and Izabela meant that three pairs of eyes should be considerably more efficient than one. With the exception of a few scallops, the coarse sand appeared barren and we found nothing.

Before long, our dive computers indicated that we would soon be needing to conduct decompression stops on the way back to the surface and since Izabela's diver grade did not allow her to do so, she ascended back up the shotline with Felicity, whilst I elected to try one more circle. I swam just inches from the sand, determined to be ready to spot the smallest of clues. Once again, I could find nothing more. Despondent, I reeled the line in as I made my way back to the bottom of the shotline. Then something caught my eye. There were two pieces of flat glass, about the size of post it notes, sticking out of the sand. They were quite encrusted with algae and barnacles, indicating that they had been there for some time. Bottle glass is a common sight on the seabed, but flat glass is not. I wondered whether to pick them up but realised that, on their own, they would tell us little, and we had already decided not to retrieve anything from the site, but they certainly added to the picture.

As I waited out my decompression time, I pictured the awful event which had happened in this place 50 years before. The fear, the panic, the screams, and then the silence. I don't mind admitting that there may have been a tear or two in my mask when I surfaced.

On the way back to Mylor we discussed what we had found. The evidence had certainly increased, but had it done so enough? Nobody wanted to be the one to jump to conclusions. As we unloaded the boat, said our goodbyes, and headed home, we were all still questioning what we had found. Apart from my dog Skipper, the house was empty when I arrived home as Julie was away at an examiner's meeting in Guildford. I had a bath, finished off the previous night's chilli and settled down in front of the television with Skipper and a glass of wine. But my mind was elsewhere. Was the wreckage the evidence we needed? Right where we had calculated the bodies had originated was where the *Darlwyne* transom had been trawled up. In the same place, we had found what looked like a granite sett, some wreckage and some window glass. And this was not part of the area searched by HMS *Iveston*. Was that enough? I mulled it over for several hours before sending Julie a text message of three words: 'Found the *Darlwyne*'.

‘The outcome of any serious research can only be to make two questions grow where only one grew before.’

Thorstein Veblen

CHAPTER 12

Questions and Answers

As our eminent archaeologist David Gibbins pointed out, this project was never likely to be a particularly diagnostic piece of archaeological investigation. That's not to say, however, that what little wreckage we discovered tells us nothing; far from it, in fact. Some of the questions which we posed at the outset remain unanswered, but we still have more pieces of the jigsaw than ever before, and a clearer picture has started to emerge. What follows are some of the questions which were written on the whiteboard above my desk as the project began, along with some of the answers for them.

Q1. Where is the wreck?

A. The evidence of the distribution of the bodies, the dredged-up transom with 'Darlwyne' painted on it and the presence of wreckage all in the same place, a location not searched by HMS *Iveston*, leads us to conclude that the wreck is in a gully to the north of the Field and Bellows reefs off Dodman Point. That is not to say that some wreckage may not be elsewhere. Having recounted the story of *UB-81* and its post-sinking voyage around the Isle of Wight, it is quite possible that some wreckage may be widely distributed. In fact, I spoke to former fisherman Martyn Rowse during the filming of the documentary, who was aboard a trawler which recovered some wreckage around six miles to the south of Dodman Point in the 1980s. Having carefully examined his information, I suspect that this is probably not from the *Darlwyne*, for reasons that will be explained (see *Chapter 13*), but the fact that the wreckage was six miles offshore would not be a factor to disqualify it.

This poses a question as to the location of the rest of the wreckage. We know that the transom was dredged up, but whether it was torn off by the dredger or already detached from the wreck is unknown. At any rate, we can be certain that the wreck was in at least two sections at some point. There is a good chance that much of the *Darlwyne* may be under the sand in the gully. The capability of sand to cover and uncover wrecks is quite phenomenal. Some time ago, Mark and I went to dive the wreck of the *SS Grip*, a small steamship carrying a cargo of salt, which ran ashore at Gunwallow Cove on the west side of the Lizard Peninsula in 1897. The wreck was reported to be mostly buried in sand with only the top of the boiler showing, but we had not previously dived it so went to take a look. We swam out from the beach and were soon greeted by an astonishing site. It was the bow of a ship. Although the superstructure had long gone, the hull, lower decks and engine room were intact. We swam the entire length of the *Grip* until we could peer over her elegant stern to see the rudder and propeller still in place. When we returned for a more detailed investigation some weeks later, the sand had returned, and she was almost totally buried. So, it may be that a great deal more of the *Darlwyne* is just where we found her, but buried in the sand.

Q2. What happened in the time between the *Darlwyne* leaving Fowey at 16.45 and her sinking at around 21.00?

A. Of course we will never know for sure. Martin Banks' theory about the boat having made some headway into Veryan Bay before the more experienced mariners in the party took over and turned her around is certainly valid, and would be so with or without the various eyewitness accounts. As I have already stated, I am not at all convinced that eyewitnesses could have identified a particular vessel at the distance claimed, especially in pouring rain and blowing spray.

Given the location of the wreck, what we know about the wind and tide on the day and the *Darlwyne*'s condition, poor stability, unsuitable engines, poor steering and gross overloading, I believe that those four hours or so were actually spent fighting against the sea just to reach Dodman Point. We know that the Dodman gave some degree of shelter from the worst of the storm but that doesn't mean that conditions in Mevagissey Bay were calm; in fact, they will still have been very rough. The speed that the *Darlwyne* would have been able to achieve would have been drastically reduced. I have taken boats infinitely more seaworthy than the *Darlwyne* out in just such conditions and have found my journey time tripled at the very least. I believe therefore, that where we found the wreckage is about as far into Veryan Bay as the *Darlwyne* actually travelled.

Q3. What caused the *Darlwyne* to sink?

A. Again, we can never know for sure, but the most significant factor must be instability. Even with the granite and pig iron ballast, the *Darlwyne*'s stability issues are well-documented. We know that there were any number of ways in which water could enter the hull with disastrous consequences and another factor came to light during the filming of the documentary. I was able to question Captain Mike Evans, formerly of the Marine Accident Investigation Branch (MAIB) of the Department of Transport. He raised the important issue of the *Darlwyne*'s fuel tanks. There were two 30-gallon fuel tanks on board. These would hold approximately a quarter of a metric ton of fuel. Since the *Darlwyne* is not known to have refuelled in Fowey, by the time she was on the return journey, the fuel level would have dropped sufficiently in the tanks for a considerable free surface effect to develop. It was just such an effect which capsized the car ferry *Herald of Free Enterprise* in Zeebrugge in 1987, with the loss of 193 lives. It took relatively little water to enter the lorry deck of the ferry, to exert extreme lateral forces as it slopped from side-to-side to destabilise the vessel. This can happen in ships' fuel tanks, too, which nowadays are fitted with baffles to prevent it. The *Darlwyne*'s tanks would not have had this feature, which can only have contributed further to a lack of stability. Obviously, the sea conditions and pre-existing stability issues are the major factors, but the sloshing fuel in the tanks was a significant destabilising force. The fact that all the recovered bodies were deep drowned, including Jean Brock who was wearing a lifebelt, strongly suggests that the vessel capsized and immediately sank, carrying the passengers and crew down with it.

Q4. Why was the line to the 16-foot skiff cut?

A. There has been much speculation about this. One suggestion was that the skiff was banging into the hull, causing damage, and was cut away to prevent this. I doubt that this was the case. We know that the passengers could not have been landed without it and it was not Brian Bown's boat anyway, so to casually dispose of someone else's boat seems unlikely. By far the easier option would have been to use a longer piece of rope, which was certainly on board the *Darlwyne.*

Another suggestion was that it was cut during an attempted evacuation of the stricken vessel. I believe this theory can be discounted for a number of reasons. Firstly, the *Darlwyne* most probably sank extremely quickly, within seconds in fact, so no such evacuation could have taken place. Again, we have the evidence that Jean Brock, who was given the only lifebelt, presumably to try to save her unborn child, was still aboard when the *Darlwyne* sank (*see page 111*). It seems reasonable to suggest that either she, or some of the children on board, would have been put into the skiff had time allowed.

Secondly, when the skiff was found, there was nobody on board and no evidence that it had ever been occupied.

Thirdly, the question of common sense. If the skiff was the means of escape from the stricken *Darlwyne*, the last thing anyone would do is cut her free from the boat. Losing the only means of escape would be totally illogical.

It seems much more reasonable to suggest that the skiff was cut free because it was acting as a sea anchor. There are occasions when a vessel will trail an object astern in order to hold the bow straight into an oncoming sea, to prevent the waves from hitting her side on. But with the *Darlwyne* struggling to make headway against the gathering storm and with her steering so poor, I suspect that the skiff was a liability that could be sacrificed in order to increase speed and manoeuvrability with a view to reaching safety.

Q5. Did Brian Bown buy the *Darlwyne*?

A. Although the Court of Inquiry was not a criminal court, this was John Barratt's defence. I have looked into this more closely and carefully than almost any other aspect of my research and can find no evidence whatsoever that supports Barratt's claim. Therefore, it seems safe to conclude that John Barratt was still the owner of the *Darlwyne* at the time of her loss.

Q6. What happened to Lisa Mills?

A. This was never a focus of the research, but the terrible, confusing situation in which she found herself is one of the most heart-rending features of the *Darlwyne* story. Lisa Mills, the three-year-old girl who stayed behind at Greatwood with her mother because she was scared of the sea, married twice and now lives in France. She was traced by Martin Banks but was emphatic that she did not wish to discuss the *Darlwyne*. I have respected her wishes and made no attempt to contact her.

Q7. In theory, could anyone have survived the sinking?

A. This question was asked frequently after the disaster. It was pointed out that, in particular, Susan Tassell and Mary Dearden were very strong swimmers and may have been able to strike out for the shore. Captain Mike Evans is quite unequivocal about this. He pointed out that although the sea is relatively warm at the end of July, it is still cold enough to severely limit survival chances. Ultimately, survival after unexpected immersion depends on the ability of the body to oxygenate its tissues. To put it simply, cold, exertion, fear and fatigue will always reduce the ability of the human body to distribute oxygen to its vital organs and muscles. Given the position of the wreck site and the conditions at the time, it is quite simply inconceivable that anyone could have survived the sinking of the *Darlwyne*.

Q8. Could an incident like this happen these days?

A. The loss of the *Darlwyne* was by no means the last disaster involving a passenger vessel in British waters. In 1989, the 46-ton pleasure boat *Marchioness* was hit by the 1,474-ton dredger *Bowbelle* near Southwark Bridge on the River Thames in London with the loss of 51 of the 131 passengers. It was concluded by the inquiry that both vessels had failed to post adequate lookouts and were using the centre of the river, and although other criticisms were levelled neither captain was ever convicted of any wrong-doing.[1] In 1966, there was already a considerable amount of legislation in place concerning the safe running of commercial vessels, which is undoubtedly the basis on which the *Darlwyne* was being run. The same can be said of 1989 when the *Marchioness* sank. Regulations will only work if they are adhered to and enforced. In both of these cases they were not. As Captain Evans stated: 'The *Darlwyne* was operating under the radar'. So, sadly, although legislation is even stricter these days, a boat operator could decide to risk ignoring it and another incident like this could always happen again.

1 Clarke, Lord Justice, Marchioness / Bowbelle Formal Investigation under the Merchant Shipping Act 1995, (2001).

‘Family connexions were always worth preserving, good company always worth seeking.’

Jane Austen

CHAPTER 13

Remembrance

Meeting Alex Scott and her family stirred mixed emotions in me. I had always felt as if there was a degree of advocacy in the *Darlwyne* project. It was as if we were, in some small way, trying to give a voice to the dead and some degree of closure for those left behind. But to finally encounter a tangible connection with the victims of the wreck was both heart-warming and oddly other-worldly. Alex Scott is the niece of Albert Russel, who was one of the first victims to be found. The Russel family had always felt a deep connection with the *Darlwyne* story which, having lost four of their family members, is hardly surprising but what I hadn't expected is that she would be accompanied by six other relatives. Her story was as poignant as any involved in the *Darlwyne* saga. Her family had been on holiday in Spain at the time and her father had bought an English newspaper to read a report of the World Cup Final. He had read about the *Darlwyne* before skipping to the back pages to find the football story. Had he simply turned the page, he would have seen the names of the victims.

Alex had been traced by Jeremy Hibbard to be featured in the documentary, in order to represent the families of the dead on the 50th anniversary of the disaster. However, this was before there was any real probability of the wreck being discovered. The whole emphasis of the documentary had now changed: to reflect the discovery of the *Darlwyne*. We had to keep the discovery secret for a few days, so that the BBC would be able to exclusively announce it via their news service as soon as some of the footage had been edited. With this in mind, it was vital that the memorial ceremony was conducted and filmed as soon as possible to be included in the news item. In the end, we took it right to the wire and held the ceremony on the 30th of July, just one day short of the anniversary.

Julie and I travelled to Mevagissey that morning to represent the dive team and help record the memorial event. It was an almost windless day, although rather overcast. We arrived early and parked on the edge of the town so that we could explore a little before everyone else arrived. As we were wandering round the inner harbour, I spotted something that brought home just how close to these small Cornish communities the *Darlwyne* story still was. There, on the slipway, sat the former RNLI lifeboat, *Gertrude*, which had been stationed at Fowey and was of the same class that had retrieved many of the *Darlwyne* victims.

As we made our way to the outer harbour, we met up with Jeremy Hibbard and cameraman Andy Johnstone, who quickly set about filming establishing shots around the picturesque harbour. Jeremy had chartered an angling boat called the *MFV Lizy* to take out to the wreck site and she was waiting for us at the bottom of the harbour steps. The skipper seemed totally unperturbed by the mountain of camera equipment, even when we were joined by Matt Burtwell, who would be filming aerial shots using a drone.

As we watched an opportunistic harbour seal casually swimming around the boat in search of a free meal, Alex and her family arrived. She was accompanied by her husband Graham, son Christopher, daughter Victoria and son-in-law James, who had also brought their children, Freddy and baby Annabel. I hadn't realised that three generations of the family would be present, but it made the whole event altogether more poignant since the age range of those who perished aboard the *Darlwyne* was perfectly, if unintentionally, represented.

As we left Mevagissey harbour, I showed the skipper where the wreck site was on the chart before joining Julie and the film crew on deck. As we chatted with the relatives, we had, for the first time, a clear sense of just what happens in a family when relatives are lost at sea. This situation actually arose within my own family when my great uncle was trapped inside the submarine *H5* when she was mistaken for a German U-boat and rammed by the British merchant ship *Rutherglen* off the coast of Wales on the 2nd of March 1918. His remains are still inside the wreck. The loss of a loved one is always a tragedy, but never being able to say a final goodbye is heart-breaking. Nowadays, of course, we call it 'closure'.

Once clear of the harbour, Matt launched his drone, a highly skilful manoeuvre considering we were aboard a moving boat festooned with aerials, antennae and rigging. Then I briefed Alex about just what we had found and where we had found it, acutely mindful that this was not just a wreck site, but very much a final resting place. After a final check with the skipper, we had reached the area just to the north of the Field and Bellows reef plateau and the engines were stopped.

I have no religious beliefs and I don't know whether Alex and her family do. Whilst there could have been prayers or blessings over the wreck site, I didn't think that the solemnity or significance of the occasion was in any way diminished by their absence. Alex gazed at the sea. Even on a windless day, the sea off the Dodman is never still and ripples lapped at the boat's stern. The moment that Alex dropped her floral wreath into the water was intensely moving. That was the emotion that closure after 50 years engenders.

I knew that Megan Hicks' favourite flowers were red tulips, but finding any at that time of year was nigh on impossible, so we had brought 31 red roses with us, one for each victim of the *Darlwyne*. As I dropped them one-by-one over the stern of the boat, the tide caught them, and they formed a stunning trail of scarlet against the dark surface of the sea. This was a moment of stark realisation. For months I had been so wrapped up in painstaking research and the minutiae of the story that, however strange it sounds, I had never really thought about just how large a number 31 was when it applied to the number of victims of a tragedy. Laying the flowers on the sea seemed to take an eternity and it was an intensely emotional experience which took me rather by surprise.

With the memorial ceremony over, we headed back to Mevagissey.

On the way a pod of dolphins swam past the boat and, in the distance, a minke whale appeared briefly ahead of the boat. I don't pretend to ascribe any symbolism to these events, but I wouldn't blame anyone who did.

Once ashore we had one more event to attend. The Mylor History Society had laid on a reception at the village hall to commemorate the 50th anniversary of the *Darlwyne*'s loss. Apart from a vast array of food and drink, the proceedings included a book reading by Martin Banks, which took on a new significance considering the relatives of the victims were in attendance.

The following day there was a special memorial service at Mylor church and, whilst the relatives attended, I decided to stay away. I felt that this was very much their occasion and I had no business being there. I had paid my respects in my way and that was enough.

It only remained to complete the filming of the documentary. On Monday the 12th of September, I met up with Jeremy Hibbard and cameraman Neil Tugwell to interview ex-fisherman, Martyn Rowse. As a young man, Martyn had been aboard a trawler which had been working some six miles south of Dodman Point. They were on their way back to port and were trawling close to a wreck in order to try to retrieve some of the boiler coal, which was a common practice amongst Cornish fishermen. As it happens they retrieved not coal, but wreckage. Various engine parts, purportedly from a Perkins P6 engine, hull and keel planking, part of a prop shaft with the oiling mechanism, and part of a helm on a steering pedestal. It was widely thought that this must have come from the *Darlwyne*, particularly as the hull planking appeared to be of double diagonal construction.

I was struggling to figure out what was going on here. Was this a spoiler? Had all our calculations been wrong and this was a surprise on the part of Jeremy to give the documentary an unexpected ending? Fortunately, I had not understood the nature of television production. It soon became clear that this sequence was to be used early in the documentary to illustrate our collaboration with local sources to try to pinpoint the wreck. The evidence was compelling but, in the end, I was able to say that this wreckage, although very similar, was very unlikely to be from the

Darlwyne. As discussed previously, it is certainly not impossible for the wreckage to be spread over a very wide area, particularly if it has been trawled across. I was pretty certain that Brian Bown would not have taken the *Darlwyne* six miles offshore, even if that is where this wreckage was found. In the end, the devil was in the detail. Martyn Rowse kindly sent me some photographs of the prop shaft oiling mechanism, which had been recycled and fitted in a home-built steam launch. It seemed much bigger than the *Darlwyne*'s. But the clincher was the steering mechanism. Close scrutiny of the plans of the *Darlwyne* revealed that the mechanism which was trawled up was very different to hers. Nevertheless, this was important evidence to consider as we could finally eliminate it and Martyn's co-operation was a valuable contribution to our research.

That afternoon saw us back at Mylor marina for the final piece of filming. Jemma Woodman, the documentary presenter, had to film all her pieces to camera and the sequences with Captain Mike Evans were recorded. Captain Evans made no bones about the *Darlwyne*'s poor condition and was adamant that she should never have put to sea, which was very much in line with our own research. He also pointed out that the very location of the wreck was the best clue as to exactly what had happened to her, which was extremely gratifying.

With the filming over and the camera and lights packed away, I took a few moments to look around. I knew Mylor so well, but that day I saw it in a different light. I looked over at Greatwood quay from where the ill-fated voyage had begun, and the imposing turrets of Greatwood House itself, protruding above the trees. I looked at the historic oyster dredging boats which still operate under sail and would certainly have been here as the *Darlwyne* motored past them. I looked at the church where the elegant memorial screen commemorates those lost in the tragedy, and I wandered into the graveyard, stopping by the Hicks' family grave, where Megan and Amanda are interred and Joel is commemorated. We had done all we could to complete their story. I wished that Megan could have been alive to receive the closure she had so badly needed. But at least now, those left behind will know that at the edge of a beautiful reef, just to the south of Dodman Point, there is somewhere that can justifiably be called the final resting place for those who were lost on the *Darlwyne*.

Postscript

The *Inside Out* documentary was broadcast on Monday the 26th of September 2016 at 7.30 pm. It proved extremely popular, gaining the highest viewing figures for a BBC South West programme that year. Even before the programme went out, the *Darlwyne* story attracted worldwide attention. Just about every major British newspaper featured the story, as well as some further afield including in the United States, Canada, Australia, and Nigeria. The diving press took a keen interest, too. A great many people who suddenly considered themselves experts on the story, decided that this couldn't possibly be the *Darlwyne* that we had found, for reasons ranging from the unlikely to the ridiculous.

But the team were unconcerned by this. We continue to socialise and dive together. We have even considered the idea of a television series. The strong, indeed overwhelming, likelihood is that what we discovered actually is the wreck site of the *Darlwyne*, but the more important fact is that the relatives and friends of those who died have a point on a map to call their loved ones' resting place. That was all we ever wanted to achieve and I'm proud to say that for their sake, we succeeded in our aim.

Glossary

admiral's barge — A small boat used often in a ceremonial capacity to transport an admiral to and from a ship.

aft — Towards the rear of a vessel.

ASDIC — Early underwater sonic submarine detection system, named after the Allied Submarine Detection Investigation Committee in 1918. Later changed to sonar.

ballast — Weight added to a vessel to increase stability.

beam — 1. The width of a vessel at its widest point. 2. Referring to wind or waves acting against the side of a vessel.

bilge keel — Small projections on a vessel's hull running longitudinally, giving extra stability.

bow — The front of a vessel.

bulkhead — A wall or partition on a vessel dividing one compartment from another.

cardinal buoy — A buoy coloured yellow and black indicating a submerged obstacle.

caulking — Material used to seal the gaps between planks on the deck and hull.

coach roof — The top of a cabin.

clinker-built — A form of ship construction in which the hull planks are overlapped giving a ridged effect.

cylinder — In diving, the tank of air or other gasses from which the diver breathes.

davit — A frame from which a lifeboat or other small boat is suspended.

decompression stop — A calculated pause during the ascent phase of a dive to allow excess absorbed nitrogen to be released from bodily tissues.

delayed surface marker buoy (DSMB) — An inflatable tube attached via string to a reel which is deployed underwater by a diver to mark their position for anyone on the surface.

displacement — A measure of a vessel's size calculated as the weight of water that would fill the space the vessel occupies.

dive computer — A computer carried by the diver which measures depth and dive time and calculates a safe profile with which to conduct the dive.

echo sounder — An instrument which measures and displays the depth and seabed beneath a vessel using a sonic beam.

galley — The cooking area on a boat or ship.

gunwale — A raised projection around the upper edge of the deck to reduce water ingress.

harbour launch — A boat for transporting goods and people around a harbour, not considered suitable for use in open sea.

keel — The lowest part of a vessel's hull.

marine plywood — Laminated wood having been additionally treated to resist damage by sea water.

nautical mile — Longer than a land mile at 6,080 feet or 1,852 metres.

neap tide — The phase of the tide during which the sea level rises and falls the least.

painter — A rope that is attached to the bow of a dinghy, or other small boat, which is used for tying up or towing.

picket boat — A small boat designed to service and defend larger vessels in port. Not designed for the open sea.

pig iron — Pieces of iron wasted as part of the casting process and used as ballast.

pilot cutter — A vessel used by the harbour pilot to guide larger vessels in and out of a port.

pinnace — An auxiliary vessel designed to service a larger ship.

port — The left side of a vessel when facing forward.

prop shaft — The propeller shaft which connects the propeller to the vessel's engine.

regulator — The device which attaches to a diver's cylinder and enables him or her to safely breathe the contents.

RIB — Rigid inflatable boat. One with inflatable side tubes and a solid hull.

Samson post — A strong upright piece of timber or metal designed to take a considerable load on a vessel.

SCUBA — Self-contained underwater breathing apparatus.

sea anchor — A device towed behind a vessel to keep her bow pointing towards the oncoming waves.

shotline — A rope with a weight at one end and a buoy at the other, used to mark a point on the seabed for divers to find.

side scan sonar — A device utilising a sonic beam to enable a horizontal representation of seabed features to be seen on a screen.

skiff — A ship's working boat used in harbour.

slack water — The period during a single tide when water movement is at its least.

spar torpedo — A bomb on the end of a pole carried by a small vessel, intended to ram an enemy vessel and detonate.

spring tide — The period during a tidal cycle in which there is greatest tidal movement.

standard dress — Old fashioned diving equipment featuring a copper or brass helmet and air hose fed from a pump on a boat or the land.

starboard — The right-hand side of a vessel when facing forward.

steam cutter — A small, steam-powered vessel.

stern — The rear of a vessel.

stringers — A part of the vessel's frame used to give additional strength.

transom — The flat end at the rear of a vessel's hull.

tidal diamond — A position marked on a nautical chart which corresponds to tidal flow information specific to that location.

wash strake — A board or barrier fitted to a vessel to prevent water splashing inboard.

weather deck — A part of the vessel's deck with no overhead protection from the elements.

web frames — Strengthening timbers between the main frame timbers of a vessel's hull.

wheelhouse — The cabin containing the steering position on a vessel.

yaw — The effect of the wind or waves to deviate a vessel from its intended course.

Acknowledgements

This project by its very nature could not possibly have been undertaken by anything less than a large and diverse team of people. They are all equally important to the story and I would like to take the opportunity to thank them here. This was a complicated trail to follow, so I apologise in advance to anyone I have accidentally omitted.

Thanks are due first to Jeremy Hibbard of Televisionary Productions. He was the first to suggest that a search for the *Darlwyne* was a viable proposition and despite my early scepticism was proved right. He produced and directed the subsequent documentary to the highest standard, ensuring that the team received not 15 but 27 minutes of fame.

The project would never have been proposed to us had Mark Milburn not had an extensive media profile as one of Cornwall's premier wreck detectives. As the owner of Atlantic Scuba dive centre near Falmouth, he had the ideal location, skills, knowledge and logistics in place to give the venture the best chance of success. I am privileged to count him amongst my best friends.

This was always going to be a needle in a haystack search, conducted far more extensively in the libraries and archives, than at sea. My thanks are due to all those who helped to shrink that haystack.

Firstly, to Martin Banks, whose previous research and writing about the *Darlwyne* proved an invaluable resource. Martin was generous with his time and knowledge during the entire project.

Without the help of two institutions in particular, I fear that the long hours spent trawling through thousands of documents, maps and newspapers would have been an insurmountable challenge. The staff at the Bartlett Maritime Research Centre offered endless advice and provided many of the sources which helped to bring the *Darlwyne* story to life. Similarly, the staff at the Cornish Studies Library in Redruth proved extremely patient with my constant requests for obscure documents which I could never have located on my own.

A core team of enthusiastic people were key to the success of the project. Andy Skentelbery's many years as a skilled boat builder give him an unparalleled knowledge of the construction of boats such as the *Darlwyne*. Julie Skentelbery played a pivotal role in allowing me to put out an appeal for information during her show on BBC Radio Cornwall, which would prove very fruitful. Thanks are also due to the numerous people who responded. The information they provided was absolutely vital.

Alex Scott represented the relatives of those who perished in the wreck. She kindly showed me archive material which had never been published before and shed new light on the tragedy.

When it came to the search itself we had a 'dream team' of wreck hunters. Dr David Gibbins is perhaps best known as a highly successful author of historical fiction, but he is also a renowned underwater archaeologist. He was more than happy not only to advise but also to get his feet wet as a search diver. The various underwater talents of Katrina Mace, Colin Stratton and Izabela Konkel proved pivotal to the search, as did the photographic skills of Felicity Flashman. Jeff Goodman is a BAFTA nominated underwater cameraman whose images, both above and below the surface, could not have told the story more clearly.

Thanks are also due closer to home. My father Robin Lyon is a lifelong sailor who was able to provide much insight into several of the more troubling nautical puzzles we encountered. My wife Julie Lyon not only spent many long hours researching in the various archives but also proofread the text as I wrote the book.

Finally, thanks are very much due to Alex Gibson of Dived Up Publications who displayed endless patience during the process of editing and publishing the book.

My sincere thanks to you all.

Index

E

F

J

K

L

M

S

T

U

V

W

Y

Z

Nick Lyon

THE DIVER'S TALE

Foreword by Andy Torbet

'It's that rare thing in diving — a very funny book'— *Diver magazine*

'A brilliant book'— Scubaverse.com

'There is no writer like the talented Mr Lyon ... I cannot recommend it highly enough'— *SCUBA*

The Diver's Tale is an unvarnished account of real British diving, based on the author's 40+ year experience. Britain is an island nation so, unsurprisingly, scuba diving is a popular British pastime enjoyed by some 50,000 keen participants and just as many of the armchair variety. A carefully-structured programme of training ensures that the British diver is well-prepared for the challenging conditions which may be encountered beneath our seas. Or does it? How many trainee divers were taught about the perils of high-speed testicular trauma during descent? Or the dangers of having sex in a tent with a deaf person? Why bacon should be in your first aid kit. How to build a space shuttle using salvaged ammunition? Or why the name Valerie is so very special? *The Diver's Tale* is not a diving manual — quite the opposite. How not to do it, why not to do it, when not to do it and who not to do it with. Amusing, frequently embarrassing, often unpleasant and occasionally tragic, the book plunges into the world of the real British diver!

'Over the years I have read a lot of diving-related books. And I mean a lot. I have to say, *The Diver's Tale* is definitely up in the top ten'— *Scuba Diver*

2nd Edn. | Paperback & ebook | ISBN 978-1-909455-24-5 | 174 pages | Feb 2019

www.DivedUp.com

CPSIA information can be obtained
at www.ICGtesting.com
Printed in the USA
LVHW070824141119
636965LV00018B/1105/P